GOD'S COUNTRY

By

Steven Dietz

SAMUEL FRENCH, INC.

45 West 25th Street   NEW YORK 10010
7623 Sunset Boulevard HOLLYWOOD 90046
LONDON   TORONTO

Copyright © 1989, 1990 by Steven John Dietz

ALL RIGHTS RESERVED

ISBN 0 573 69158 4   Printed in U.S.A.

IMPORTANT BILLING AND CREDIT
REQUIREMENTS

All producers of GOD'S COUNTRY *must* give credit to the Author of the Play in all programs distributed in connection with performances of the Play and in all instances in which the title of the Play appears for purposes of advertising, publicizing or otherwise exploiting the Play and/or a production. The name of the Author *must* also appear on a separate line, on which no other name appears, immediately following the title, and *must* appear in size of type not less than fifty percent the size of the title type.

This play is dedicated to the memory of Alan Berg

ACKNOWLEDGMENTS

The author wishes to thank the following organizations and individuals whose expertise and support led to the creation of *God's Country:*

David Eugene Wilson, Susan Barnes, Peter Mueller – U.S. District Attorney's office, Seattle

The Kootenai County Task Force on Human Relations

The Center for Democratic Renewal

The Southern Poverty Law Center

The Youth Project, Minneapolis

A Contemporary Theatre, Seattle

The Playwrights' Center

New York Stage & Film Company

Anath White

Jannie Harper

Leslie Ball

Gwynneth Gibby

Minnesota State Arts Board

Theatre Communications Group

God's Country was commissioned by and received its world premiere at A Contemporary Theatre in Seattle; Jeff Steitzer, Artistic Director. It was directed by David Ira Goldstein. The set was designed by Shelley Henze Schermer, the lighting by Phil Schermer, the costumes by Frances Kenny, and the sound by Jim Ragland. The dramaturg was Steven E. Alter. The stage manager was Craig Weindling.

The cast was as follows:

ACTOR ONE	John Aylward
ACTOR TWO	Marianne Owen
ACTOR THREE	John Gilbert
ACTOR FOUR	Linda Emond
ACTOR FIVE	Rex McDowell
ACTOR SIX	Anne Christianson
ACTOR SEVEN	Kurt Beattie
ACTOR EIGHT	Michael Winters
ACTOR NINE	Gordon Carpenter
ACTOR TEN	Ben Prager
BOY	Matthew Flemming

This production ran from August 18 to September 11, 1988.

God's Country was subsequently produced by Actors Theatre of Louisville as part of their 1989 Humana Festival of New American Plays. This production was directed by the author. The set was designed by Paul Owen, the lighting by Ralph Dressler, the costumes by Lew Rampino, and the sound by Mark Hendren. The stage manager was Debra Acquavella.

The cast was as follows:

ACTOR ONE	Andy Backer
ACTOR TWO	Mary Boucher
ACTOR THREE	David Little
ACTOR FOUR	Lizbeth Mackay
ACTOR FIVE	Chris Wells
ACTOR SIX	Joanne Manley
ACTOR SEVEN	Edward Hyland
ACTOR EIGHT	Bob Morrisey
ACTOR NINE	Jonathan Fried
ACTOR TEN	James Macdonald
BOY	Jonathan Davidson

The production ran from March 9 to April 1, 1989

CHARACTERS

ACTOR ONE (man, 50's)
Farrell, retired Air Force colonel
Phillips, attorney for David Lane
Pastor One
Savage, attorney for Andrew Barnhill
Father
Detective Kerber
David Lane, defendant

ACTOR TWO (woman, 40's)
Leatherman, attorney for Randy Duey
Judith Berg

ACTOR THREE (man, 40's)
Alan Berg, radio talk show host
Candidate
Mister Jones, conspiratologist
Ruark, attorney for Bruce Pierce

ACTOR FOUR (woman, 30's)
Mueller, prosecuting attorney
Wife of the Farmer

ACTOR FIVE (man, 30's)
Denver Parmenter, witness for the
prosecution
Candidate

ACTOR SIX (woman, 20's)
 Zillah Craig, mistress
 Student
 Anath White, radio producer
 Ms. Wiggins, neighbor of Alan Berg

ACTOR SEVEN (man, 30's)
 Elliot, publisher
 Ward, prosecuting attorney
 Pastor Two
 Robinson, prosecuting attorney
 Randall Rader, witness for the prosecution
 Dr. Ogura, coroner's pathologist
 Gary Lee Yarbrough, defendant

ACTOR EIGHT (man, 30's)
 Chappel, attorney for Jean Craig
 Farmer
 Pastor Three
 Peter Lake, filmmaker
 Mister Smith, conspiratologist
 Thomas Martinez, witness for the prosecution
 Bruce Pierce, defendant

ACTOR NINE (man, 20's)
 Halprin, attorney for Ardie McBrearty
 Candidate
 Patrick Connor, promotion assistant
 Officer Phelan

ACTOR TEN (man, late 20's)
Robert Jay Mathews, martyr
Candidate
Skinhead

BOY (10-12 years old)
As noted

A Note On Using An Additonal Actor

In the Oregon Shakespeare Festival production of the play, one additional male actor was added to the cast, creating, therefore, ACTOR ELEVEN. The advantage of this decision is that it gives more focus to the role of Alan Berg and, to a lesser extent, the roles of Denver Parmenter and Robert Jay Mathews – because the actors playing these roles (ACTOR THREE, ACTOR FIVE and ACTOR TEN) are required to do less doubling into other roles.

TIME and PLACE

1983 to the present

A Seattle courtroom, a Denver radio station, and numerous other locations across the United States.

GOD'S COUNTRY

ACT I

Anyone who has the power
to make you believe absurdities
has the power to make you
commit injustices.

Voltaire

SCENE: A large spacious performing arena. Powerful. Airy.

Ten small shafts of vertical light which form a circle on the stage.

A bench in the center of this circle.

Other benches at the perimeter of the playing area.

Small units will be brought on to serve as pulpits, radio console, etc.

Numerous banners, flags and photos will fly in from the grid.

The primary transformation of the stage will be done through lighting. The lighting should be specific and aggressive.

AT RISE: Darkness. Silence.

LIGHTS reveal the CAST scattered about the stage. THEY watch the BOY as HE enters, carrying a white candle. The BOY arrives at the center bench and stops, facing the audience. HE puts his hand over his heart.

BOY. I pledge allegiance. To the flag. Of the United States of America.

ACTOR ONE. U.S. District Court. Seattle, Washington. 1985.

MUELLER. The government calls Mr. Denver Parmenter.

(*The CAST exits. LIGHTS reveal MUELLER and PARMENTER. During the following, the BOY ceremonially lights three candles on the center bench.*)

MUELLER. Mr. Parmenter, when you started college at Cheney in eastern Washington, did you have any particular political view of any kind?

PARMENTER. Yes. At that time I had pretty much what you refer to as a conservative point of view, or right wing. Very much in support of Ronald Reagan's candidacy.

MUELLER. Over the years you were at Cheney, did your views change in any way?

PARMENTER. Yes, they did. They became more to the extreme right and eventually became very radical.

MUELLER. Did there come a time in the summer of 1981 when you became aware of a group located nearby in Idaho by the name of Aryan Nations?

PARMENTER. Yes.

MUELLER. How did you react to your first visit at Aryan Nations?

PARMENTER. Very positively. Talked to Pastor Butler who was the pastor of the church.

MUELLER. Mr. Parmenter, was there anything different about the philosophy or beliefs

that you encountered in the Aryan Nations as
opposed to the right wing views you had held before
you went up there?

PARMENTER. Yes. It basically brought a
form of Christianity into the overall philosophy of
the right wing, and the fact that the white race was
considered to be the true Israelites of the Bible.

MUELLER. Is there a shorthand name for that
belief that you are aware of?

PARMENTER. Identity. Normally referred
to as the Identity Doctrine.

MUELLER. Directing your attention to
approximately September of 1983. Did there come
a time when you began discussing, with Robert
Jay Mathews, future political activities of any
kind?

PARMENTER. Yes. We came to discuss the
white movement's non-activity as far as actually
doing some of the things we had been talking
about, and we began to discuss the possibility of
setting up an organization to begin showing force.

MUELLER. What action did you take in that
respect?

PARMENTER. Bob Mathews decided to form
the organization and he got some people together
and we met.

MUELLER. What happened at the meeting?

PARMENTER. Bob had a set of goals and
objectives for us. We agreed upon them. We took
an oath and formed The Order.

MUELLER. Did the name The Order come from any particular publication that you were aware of?

PARMENTER. Probably *The Turner Diaries*.

MUELLER. What were *The Turner Diaries* as you understood them?

PARMENTER. *The Turner Diaries* was a book written by William Pierce under a pen name and it was basically the blueprint to revolution by the white movement.

MUELLER. You said Mr. Mathews had a outline of goals that he presented to the group?

PARMENTER. Yes. They were referred to as Steps. The first two I'm not really sure of. They were just like forming the group, setting the goals. But the Third Step was the War Chest.

MUELLER. Meaning what?

PARMENTER. Acquiring money to finance the group. Robberies basically were stressed as the most viable way.

MUELLER. What was Step Four?

PARMENTER. Step Four was recruiting members for the organization.

MUELLER. Was there a Step Five?

PARMENTER. Yes. Step Five was assassinations.

(*ACTOR ONE, ACTOR THREE, ACTOR SEVEN, ACTOR EIGHT, ACTOR NINE and ACTOR TEN enter and stand in a circle*

*around the bench, where the candles are
burning.
The BOY backs away, watching.
The MEN wear rugged clothing, some in
camouflaged fatigues, some with weapons.
ACTOR TEN places a baby, bundled in a blanket,
on the bench.)*

MUELLER. (*As the MEN gather.*) Now, you
mentioned that this initial meeting involved the
taking of an oath?

PARMENTER. Yes.

MUELLER. Would you describe what
occurred in that respect?

PARMENTER. Yes. We all gathered in a
circle. A child, a baby, was placed in the middle of
the circle as a symbol of our race, the future of our
race, of what we were fighting for. Bob Mathews
normally would recite the oath and we would
repeat it after him.

(*PARMENTER, like the BOY, turns and watches
the MEN. The oath is urgent and aggressive,
not solemn.*)

ACTOR TEN. I, as a free Aryan man, hereby
swear an unrelenting oath upon the green graves
of our sires —

ACTOR ONE. Upon the children in the wombs
of our wives —

ACTOR NINE. Upon the throne of God Almighty —

ALL MEN. (*Except Parmenter.*) Sacred be his name.

ACTOR THREE. To join together in holy union with those brothers in this circle —

ACTOR EIGHT. And to declare forthright that from this moment on I have no fear of death —

ACTOR SEVEN. No fear of foe —

ACTOR TEN. That I have a sacred duty to do whatever is necessary to deliver our people from the Jew —

ACTOR ONE. And bring total victory to the Aryan race.

MUELLER. Mr. Parmenter, you say you were in and out of Aryan Nations. Why was that?

PARMENTER. Because of the situation with my wife.

ACTOR SEVEN. I, as an Aryan warrior, swear myself to complete secrecy to The Order —

ACTOR THREE. And total loyalty to my comrades.

PARMENTER. My wife did not agree with the philosophy of Aryan Nations.

ALL MEN. Let me bear witness to you, my brothers —

ACTOR NINE. That should one of you fall in battle, I will see to the welfare and well-being of your family.

PARMENTER. Plus, I was having drinking problems.

ALL MEN. Let me bear witness to you, my brothers —

ACTOR TEN. That should one of you be taken prisoner, I will do whatever is necessary to regain your freedom.

PARMENTER. I was trying to satisfy my wife and also satisfy my own personal beliefs.

ALL MEN. Let me bear witness to you, my brothers —

ACTOR THREE. That should an enemy agent hurt you —

ACTOR ONE. I will chase him to the ends of the earth —

ACTOR EIGHT. And remove his head from his body.

MUELLER. On the occasion of the first meeting of The Order, was your wife present?

PARMENTER. Yes.

MUELLER. And your child?

PARMENTER. Yes.

ALL MEN. Let me bear witness to you, my brothers —

ACTOR TEN. That if I break this oath, let me be forever cursed upon the lips of our people as a coward.

ACTOR SIX. (*Appearing in a shaft of LIGHT.*) And what occurred with your child with reference to the oath?

PARMENTER. Bob Mathews wanted to use my child to be placed in the center of the circle.

ACTOR ONE. My brothers, let us be his battle axe and weapons of war.

PARMENTER. My wife refused.

ACTOR NINE. Let us go forth by ones and by twos —

ACTOR THREE. By scores and by legions —

ACTOR SIX. What was your reaction to it?

ACTOR EIGHT. And as true Aryan men with pure hearts and strong minds —

PARMENTER. It was somewhat embarrassing to me.

ACTOR SEVEN. Face the enemies of our faith and our race with courage and determination.

ACTOR TWO. (*Appearing in a shaft of LIGHT.*) How did you feel about your child being placed in the center of the circle?

ALL MEN. We hereby invoke the blood covenant, and declare that we are in a full state of war and will not lay down our weapons until we have driven the enemy into the sea, and reclaimed that land which was promised to our fathers of old —

MUELLER. Did you have any strong emotional feeling about a child being in the center of the circle?

ALL MEN. And through our blood and His will, becomes the land of our children to be.

PARMENTER. I felt it would be an honor to have my child in the middle of the circle.

ACTOR TEN. (*Holding the baby toward the sky.*) Hail Victory!

ALL MEN. HAIL VICTORY!

(*Fast BLACKOUT.*
*MUSIC: First verse and chorus of U2's "In God's Country."**
LIGHTS reveal BERG sitting at a small console containing a microphone and phone bank. HE sips coffee. Smokes.
MUSIC FADES as BERG speaks.)

BERG. Wait a minute, how can you think I'm wonderful? Let's get back to someone who really hates me. All lines are open. 861-TALK. 861-8255. You're on the air.

ACTOR NINE. (*In shaft of LIGHT.*) Just calm down a little bit.

BERG. No. I will never calm down so long as people think this stupidly and resolve issues based on no factuality. I'm always going to get — I hope I never quit getting angry.

ACTOR NINE. Oh, definitely get angry, but try to be a little more subtle and —

BERG. Give me an example. Isn't that how the Jews got theirs in Nazi Germany? By being, you know, by saying *they really don't mean it?*

ACTOR NINE. No, you have to stand up and say what you want to say —

---

* See Production Note on page 165.

BERG. The era of the Jew taking a backseat to anyone is over, dear, and the next Jew that does will get annihilated by mentalities like the people that talked on this show.

(*Shaft of LIGHT on ACTOR TWO. SHE speaks to the audience.*)

ACTOR TWO. In 1983, Alan Berg was working at KOA radio in Denver. He was the most notorious on-air personality working at the West's most powerful station. He was Jewish, he was liberal, he was bright and he was outspoken. A bleeding heart with an acid tongue. At fifty years of age, the former Chicago lawyer had earned the nickname, "The Last Angry Man." One listener said: "He had the ability to manipulate people into saying what they really wanted to say. That can be dangerous."

(*LIGHTS reveal ELLIOT and FARRELL.*)

BERG. See, when you make these indictments against the Jews, Mr. Farrell, one of the really *nice* things would be to have some *facts* available, and the facts *are* available if you care to look at them.

FARRELL. We'd like to sit down and debate them with you.

ACTOR TWO. On June 15th, 1983, Berg's program linked up via telephone with two avowed white supremacists: Rick Elliott, publisher of the *Primrose and Cattleman's Gazette*, which ran such articles as "The Death of the White Race," and retired Air Force Colonel Bud Farrell. The show was prompted by the fact that U.S. Representative Patricia Schroeder had discovered the U.S. Marine Corps to be advertising in the *Gazette*. It was rumored that, using her position on the House Armed Services Committee, she had the ads stopped.

BERG. Well, it's so *simple*. In fact, it would be far more valuable for you to write, let's say, the Holocaust Museum. Write, let's see, the United Jewish Federation. They'll send you all the information you want, with all the documentation, with the names of the Jews who died in World War II. They *documented* this. This is not a *game*. This is not *made up*. This is *reality*. I would be the first to tell you that if we say six million — you know, somebody could have made a *mistake*. It could be five. It could be four. In fact, it could be seven.

ELLIOTT. It could also be two.

BERG. Well, is that really the issue, Mr. Elliott?

ELLIOTT. That is not the issue, except that you people are *making* it the issue — to try to say why Pat Schroeder did what she did.

BERG. I think Pat Schroeder was *wrong*. I dramatically disagree with her. I think Pat Schroeder owes us a phone call on this one. She's a lady I've long admired. Hey, I took a pretty good pie in the face from Pat Schroeder once, at a fund raiser. So, for the pie in the face I could get a call on this one.

ELLIOTT. She is saying we are anti-Semitic when that is not a fact.

BERG. Sir, that speaks for itself in the very comments you're making. You're not anti-Semitic. You're anti-Jewish.

ELLIOTT. I AM NOT AND I –

BERG. You're accusing the Jews of a world conspiracy to take away your Christianity! That is not exactly a *love affair* with Jews, is it?

FARRELL. Alan, let me ask you a question. You're not married?

BERG. Fortunately for the women out there I'm not.

FARRELL. Say you're married. Now, could you be loyal to a wife and a girlfriend? How can you explain dual citizenship, then? How can you explain dual loyalty?

BERG. I don't think it's difficult to explain at all –

FARRELL. You've got a country that's in trouble, the economy is in trouble –

BERG. Are you familiar with *Israel's* economy?

FARRELL. Well, there's hyper-inflation.

BERG. How much inflation?

FARRELL. I know it's much greater than ours.

BERG. Would you perceive the Jew of Israel as a rich person?

FARRELL. (*Reading from a card ELLIOTT has handed him.*) The figures I have say that every family in Israel got over ten thousand four hundred dollars of U.S. taxpayers' money

BERG. That's the most fallacious — sir, you will never see more collective poverty and merely getting along than you will in Israel. I would urge you to take a *trip* to Israel, or to look at how the average Israeli *lives*. They're living hand-to-mouth. Are you familiar with that?

ELLIOTT. I'm familiar with hand-to-mouth, but again we're getting to the point of what we're talking about —

BERG. But see, you accused the Jewish banker of this conspiracy and here is the state of Israel barely getting along. It's *unbelievable*. You have to *be there* to see it. Let me urge you again, all right? If you want some *facts*, instead of whistling Dixie here —

ELLIOTT. I AM NOT WHISTLING DIXIE.

BERG. You're whistling it because everything you have said is a *lie*, okay? But I think you have a right to advance your lies. I'm still protecting your *right to lie*, okay? As long as you lie, I like it open like this because, you see, you have no *facts*. You have *made up* and you have *inferred a thought,* like all fanatics. Like John Birchers, like Klansmen, like all these folks.

ELLIOTT. You're crazy.

BERG. *I'm* crazy, sir. *You're* a healthy person. Thanks so much for calling.

(*BERG pushes a button on the console. LIGHTS out on FARRELL and ELLIOTT.*
MUSIC: "Small Town" [acoustic version] by John Cougar Mellencamp.*
LIGHTS shift to the FARMER, standing beside a small table which is cluttered with newspapers. His WIFE sits at the table, cutting articles out of the papers and filing them in a small, wooden box. THEY each have coffee mugs. MUSIC FADES as the FARMER speaks to the audience.)

FARMER. Yeah, I know. You're above this, right? I know. I remember.

Six months ago you stood at that window with a cup of coffee in your hand. You stood there waiting for the Sheriff – a man you sit next to at church – waiting for him to serve you the papers. At that moment, you have two pictures in your head: Your grandfather showing you around the farm for the first time when you were a kid. And your son finding you in the barn with the gun loaded and cocked. You're standing there, waiting to give four generations away.

---

* See Production Note on page 165.

Up the road comes a couple pickups you don't recognize. Men get out. Five of them. Dressed like you. Carrying rifles. They knock on your door and you open it. "We've heard they're tryin' to take your farm away from you." You nod. They position themselves in front of your door, rifles in hand, as the Sheriff pulls up. The Sheriff takes a step toward your farmhouse. The five rifles take aim at his face. One of the men you do not know says: "This is an illegal seizure of this man's personal property. As citizens at war with an occupational government, we refuse to acknowledge the authority of the county to confiscate this man's farm." You suspect the Sheriff's reaction to be the same as yours: What the hell is this? The Sheriff takes another step and begins to speak again. As he does, one of the other men puts it a different way: "Take one more step and we'll blow your fucking head off your shoulders. Is that clear?" The Sheriff looks you in the eye, turns and leaves. As the men lower their rifles, you begin — out of what? habit? instinct? — to thank them. Invite them in. But they are already climbing back in their pickups. You ask their names and they say they'll be in touch. They drive away leaving behind the words "illegal seizure," "occupational government," and "citizens at war." You're left standing in your yard as your kids rush out the door and head for school.

You begin to *pay attention*. The news looks different to you now. As does your land. And your son. And your God. You're not an evil man. You have found refuge. Somewhere between the evening news and the Sunday sermon, you have found your country. Your hatred has become your logic. You've turned a corner. Haven't you?

(*MUSIC: The chorus of "Maxwell's Silver Hammer" by the Beatles.**
LIGHTS fade on the FARMER and his WIFE. LIGHTS linger for a moment on the BOY, who has watched the previous scene from another part of the stage. LIGHTS shift to the ten shafts of vertical light which form a circle. During the following, the ACTORS one by one fill the ten shafts of light.)

ACTOR ONE. July, 1985. In a courtroom guarded by 18 armed U.S. Marshals, the criminal enterprise known as The Order is brought to trial. The defendants' chairs are bolted to the floor, and machine guns are hidden throughout the courtroom to be used in the event of a riot.

ACTOR FIVE. Several former Order members, including Denver Parmenter, accept plea agreements and testify against the other defendants in exchange for leniency.

---

* See Production Note on page 165.

ACTOR ONE. The government brings racketeering charges against nine men and one woman. They are:

*(SLIDE: RICHARD KEMP
        "HAMMER")*

ACTOR SEVEN. Richard Kemp. Twenty-two. Known to his fellow Order members as "Hammer." They liked to play a well-known Beatles song in his honor. Kemp earned the name "Hammer" after the group decided something must be done with their friend Walter West, who had trouble remaining both sober and secretive. Under the guise of inducting West into The Order, Kemp and three others walked him into the woods. Kemp took a hammer and shattered West's skull. When West, still conscious, cried out "What's going on?" he was shot in the head with his own gun and placed in a shallow grave. His brains were retrieved and buried with the body.

*(SLIDE: RANDY DUEY
        "LUKE")*

ACTOR SIX. Randy Duey. Thirty-four. The man who coolly finished off Walter West with a round of bullets. After this incident, Duey was given the name "Luke," based on a Paul Newman movie.

(SLIDE: BRUCE PIERCE
"BRIGHAM")

ACTOR NINE. Bruce Pierce. Thirty. Called "Brigham" due to his strange resemblance to Morman founder, Brigham Young.

(SLIDE: GARY YARBROUGH
"YOSEMITE SAM")

ACTOR EIGHT. Gary Yarbrough. Thirty. The only defendant with a previous criminal record. His red hair and mustache earned him the name "Yosemite Sam."

(SLIDE: FRANK SILVA
"STERLING")

ACTOR TEN. Frank Silva. Twenty-seven. Known as "Sterling." He operated The Order's secret message center.

(SLIDE: JEAN CRAIG
"RAINY")

ACTOR FOUR. Jean Craig. Fifty-seven. The only woman defendant. She did surveillance for the group and was the mother of Robert Mathews' twenty year-old mistress, Zillah. Jean Craig was called "Rainy" because of her tendency to burst into tears.

(SLIDE: RANDALL EVANS
       "CALVIN")

ACTOR TWO. Randall Evans. Twenty-nine. A former California Klan member who helped plan The Order's most successful robbbery. He was called "Calvin" for no apparent reason.

(SLIDE: ANDREW BARNHILL
*   "MR. CLOSET")*

ACTOR THREE. Andrew Barnhill. Twenty-eight. A former member of CSA — the Covenant, Sword and Arm of the Lord. Barnhill was called "Mr.Closet" based on a remark he made when asked where members of the opposite sex should be kept.

(SLIDE: ARDIE McBREARTY
*   "THE PROFESSOR")*

ACTOR FIVE. Ardie McBrearty. Fifty-seven. Though he went to great lengths during the trial to deny it, McBrearty was known as "The Professor." He created the homemade Voice Stress Analyzer Test which was given to Order recruits to be certain of their loyalty.

(SLIDE: DAVID LANE
*   "LONE WOLF")*

ACTOR ONE. And David Lane. Forty-eight. The often brilliant, often brooding former Denver Klan leader. He was known as "Lone Wolf."

VOICE OF COURT/ACTOR FIVE *(On tape.)* Opening statements. Mr.Ward.

(The ACTORS break the circle. WARD and
MUELLER – the prosecutors – occupy one side
of the stage. CHAPPEL, PHILLIPS,
HALPRIN, RUARK and LEATHERMAN –
defense attorneys – occupy another part of the
stage.)

WARD. *(Addresses the audience/jury.)*
Thank you, Your Honor. I am one of six U.S.
attorneys who will prosecute this case on behalf of
the government. Now, you are going to hear the
name Robert Mathews an awful lot during this
case. Robert Mathews is no longer living. He died
last December on Whidbey Island.

(SLIDE: Photo of ROBERT JAY MATHEWS, with
his name as a caption.
MATHEWS enters. The BOY sits nearby,
holding a football. Mathews wears a sweater,
jeans and boots. HE carries a book.
MATHEWS speaks to the audience. HE is
calm, charming and persuasive. During the
following, HE moves to the BOY and gives
him a book. The BOY puts down the football
and reads from the book. The trial becomes a
tableau.)

MATHEWS. I soon settled down to marriage,
clearing my land, and reading. Reading became
an obsession with me. I consumed volume upon
volume on subjects dealing with history, politics

and economics. My knowledge of ancient European history started to awaken a wrongfully suppressed emotion buried deep within my soul. That of racial pride and consciousness. The stronger the love for my people grew, the deeper became my hatred for those who would destroy my race, my heritage. The more I came to love my son, the more I realized that unless things changed radically, by the time he was my age, he would be a stranger in his own land. I came to learn that this was not by accident. That there is a small, cohesive group within this nation working day and night to make this happen. A secret war has been developing between the regime in Washington, and an ever growing number of people who are determined to regain what our forefathers discovered, explored, conquered and died for. Until now, we have been doing nothing more than growing and preparing. The government, however, seems determined to force the issue.

(*MATHEWS exits. The BOY also exits, reading the book. The trial tableau breaks.*)

WARD. There is simply no question that Mathews was the founder and leader of this group called The Order. These defendants, each and every defendant in this case, at various times during late 1983 or '84 joined the movement. There will be evidence that to a certain extent this group patterned itself after the racist group in a book known as *The Turner Diaries*.

CHAPPEL. My client objects.

HALPRIN. So do I, Your Honor.

VOICE OF COURT/ACTOR FIVE. (*On mike.*) This is an opening statement. It is not evidence in the case. The jury has been so advised.

WARD. The government expects to prove each and every count that's set forth in the indictment.

VOICE OF COURT/ACTOR FIVE. Mr. Chappel.

CHAPPEL. Thank you. I represent Jean Craig. She is the one woman in this case. The evidence is going to show that Jean Craig was not a young militant. The evidence, ladies and gentlemen, is going to show that The Order was a man's world and a woman did not have a voice. What this case is centered on is the testimony of a few people who have entered into what the government will call plea agreements. What those really are are plea *bargains*. You give me what I want and I'll give you what you want. Ladies and gentlemen, these witnesses are merely *puppets* of the government. *Toys*. There will be strings from the hands, strings from the head, hinges on the jaws. One of the things the government has talked about is the death of Alan Berg, the Denver disc jockey. He died, ladies and gentlemen, in a Mafia-style execution. The evidence is going to show that Alan Berg was one of the most hated men in America, and that there were many people who may have wanted to kill him. I want to talk about Whidbey Island. The government has indicated in its opening statement that Robert Mathews died in a fire. The government has not told you much about the *evidence* of what happened on Whidbey Island — but this is what the evidence is going to show: that the FBI killed Robert Mathews.

WARD. Your Honor, I object. There is no such evidence. Mr. Chappel knows that.

VOICE OF COURT/ACTOR FIVE. Again, it is an opening statement. It is not evidence of any kind. Mr. Phillips.

PHILLIPS. Thank you, Your Honor. I am the attorney for David Lane. No one is on trial for what they said or what they wrote. Nobody is on trial for their beliefs.

VOICE OF COURT/ACTOR FIVE. Mr. Halprin.

HALPRIN. I am involved in this defense with Ardie McBrearty. The government is going to suggest that these people are neo-Nazis, but they are *not* going to mention that Mr. McBrearty volunteered in World War II to fight *against* the Nazis. The government is going to suggest that Mr. McBrearty and others here are racists. They are *not* going to tell you that during the time he has been in prison, he has been teaching a Bible class to *blacks* and *Hispanics*. You have heard that The Order frowned very heavily on race mixing.

Well, Mr. McBrearty's son is married to a
Filipino woman, an *Asian*. They have two
children, Mr. McBrearty's grandchildren, who
are *half-Filipino*. Very curious behavior for a
racist. Very curious, indeed. The FACT is that
Mr. McBrearty wasn't even contacted by any of
the people who have been involved with this whole
mess until *after* all the *big, exciting* crimes had
already been committed. What is going on here?
The government's idea is to make all these people
into one group. They're hoping that after you have
sat through oh, two, three hundred witnesses that
none of the individual defendants will stand out
in any way. A person accused of *murder* will
begin to seem *morally identical* to someone
accused of walking across a state line with some
money. The efforts of the government will be a
little like tuna fishing. You take a boat out into the
ocean. You drop your nets outs. And whatever
happens to come up – whether it's a *big* tuna or a
small tuna, or if it is a *dolphin* that normally
swims in the same waters – the fisherman makes
no attempt to separate the dolphins from the tuna,
the baby tuna from the adult tuna. It all ends up in
the same net.

(*MUSIC INTRO begins.*)

HALPRIN. It all ends up equally dead.

(MUSIC: "See That My Grave is Kept Clean" by
*   Bob Dylan.* * *Intro, verse one and verse two.*
LIGHTS shift. Very dark stage. Trace of
*   MOONLIGHT. Shadows.*
A woman – ACTOR TWO – enters, dressed for
*   the cold. SHE carries a small notebook and a*
*   flashlight, which SHE shines on the ground as*
*   SHE moves about the stage. SHE is inscribing*
*   names from tombstones. She is joined by*
*   ACTOR SIX. THEY recite the following lists*
*   softly as the MUSIC PLAYS and the dialogue*
*   between MUELLER and PARMENTER is*
*   heard.)*

ACTOR TWO.	ACTOR SIX.
Charles Lee Austin.	Michael Harris.
William Alan Rogers.	Monte Ross Sharpe.
Scott Adam Walker.	Richard Black.
Roger L. Morton.	Steve J. Lewis.
Michael Schmidt.	Bette Wilder.
Lyle Dean Nash.	Patrick Deberio..
Floyd Shaw.	Richard O'Connor.
Billie Salisbury.	Richard Jennings.
Scott William Allgood.	Eric Hartman.
David Zimmerman.	Gladys Engstrom.

---

* See Production Note on page 165.

Mark Edward	Mathew Mark
Raymond.	Samuels.
Ann Payne.	Tom D. Benjamin.
Patrick LaRouche.	Pat Stone.
(Repeat and continue until noted ...)	*(Repeat and continue until noted ...)*

VOICE OF MUELLER. (*On mike, overlapping.*) At this meeting with Mr. Mathews in Boise, did he show you anything that related to obtaining false identification?

PARMENTER. (*In shaft of LIGHT.*) Yes, he did. He showed us a list of — quite an extensive list of names of dead babies that was acquired for the use of getting I.D.

VOICE OF MUELLER. Did he explain where the list had come from?

PARMENTER. Yes. He said that the girls had acquired it, had done the groundwork for it.

VOICE OF MUELLER. How would the names be acquired?

PARMENTER. By going to graveyards and, I assume — that was one of the ways we did it — by going to graveyards and getting the names off the tombstones.

VOICE OF MUELLER. And once you had the name of an infant who had died, what would you do with it?

(*ACTOR FOUR joins the other WOMEN in the graveyard.*)

ACTOR TWO.	ACTOR SIX.	ACTOR FOUR.
(Repeat and continue.)	*(Repeat and continue.)*	Chad W. Singer Bruce William Fry.
ACTOR TWO.	ACTOR SIX.	ACTOR FOUR.
(Repeat and continue.)	*(Repeat and continue.)*	Edgar Lynn Williams. Dana Swift Nelson. William Lee Rose. Scott McEveland. Keith Alan Merwin. Andrew Smith. Wyatt Hunter. Molley Bradley. Robert Sterling. Dan White.

PARMENTER. (*Overlapping.*) The name of the dead infant would be used to acquire a death certificate, and once we got the death certificate,

the vital information we needed to get the birth
certificate was provided to us.

(*LIGHTS out on PARMENTER.*
*ACTOR TWO and ACTOR FOUR sit and
consider their lists under the LIGHT of their
flashlights.*
ACTOR SIX turns and speaks to the audience.
MUSIC FADES.)

ACTOR SIX. When President John F.
Kennedy was shot and killed, I was six years old.
My Sunday school teacher was named Mr.
Oswald. This confused me. I was confused
because this man had shot the President, but was
allowed to lead my Sunday school class in prayer.
I thought someone would say something. I thought
one of the parishioners would say: You know,
since Mr.Oswald shot the President, perhaps he
should not be on our payroll any longer. But he
was there. John 3:16. John 3:16.

He was always very nice during Sunday
school. He had a soft voice and crooked teeth and
he let us eat pretzels. He looked different than he
did on television. As the next Sunday approached,
I was worried because I hadn't learned the Bible
passage I'd been assigned. Instead, I was sitting
on the floor of my parents' bedroom, holding my
baby brother, watching television. I saw Mr.
Oswald. I saw Mr. Oswald being taken away in
handcuffs. I thought, maybe I won't have to learn

my Bible passage. Then he got shot. I watched it. They said he was dead. I laid my baby brother on the bed and I learned my Bible passage by heart.

And the following Sunday, Mr. Oswald was there again, teaching us how to pray. Still no one said anything: You know, since Mr. Oswald shot and killed the President and then was gunned down on national television, maybe he should be relieved of his Sunday school duties. But he was there. John 3:16. John 3:16.

To this day, I believe in eternal life.

(*MUSIC: A boy's choir singing "America, the Beautiful."*
LIGHTS shift.
During the following litany of names, three pulpits are set up. Large flags unfurl behind the pulpits.
PASTOR ONE stands behind the center pulpit, wearing the Aryan Nations uniform – light blue shirt, dark blue pants, dark blue tie, and arm patch. Behind him is the Aryan Nations flag.
PASTOR TWO stands behind his pulpit wearing an expensive, fashionable suit, and a Nazi armband. Behind him is the flag of Hitler's Third Reich.
PASTOR THREE stands behind his pulpit wearing an open-collared shirt, sleeves rolled up. Behind him is the Ku Klux Klan flag.)

VOICE OF PARMENTER. Step Four was recruiting members for the organization. We were hoping we could recruit members from the various right wing organizations, such as the Klan, other Identity churches, any right-wing movement we could find that would be helpful.

ACTOR TWO. The list reads like a litany.

(*The list of organizations is done urgently, a cacophony of names, as the ACTORS fill the stage.*)

ACTOR THREE. American Nazi Party.

ACTOR TEN. Arizona Patriots. Aryan Brotherhood.

ACTOR FIVE. Aryan Nations.

ACTOR SIX. Aryan Youth Movement.

ACTOR TWO. Groups that espouse violence.

ACTOR NINE. Bruder Schweigen Task Force II.

ACTOR FOUR. Chicago Area Skinheads.

ACTOR TWO. Groups that denounce the I.R.S.

ACTOR TEN. Christian Patriots Defense League.

ACTOR THREE. Church of the Creator.

ACTOR TEN. Civilian Material Assistance.

ACTOR THREE. Confederate Strike Force Skinheads. Confederate Vigilante Knights.

ACTOR TWO. Groups that harass and intimidate.

ACTOR FOUR. Covenant, Sword and Arm of the Lord.

ACTOR FIVE. Duck Club.

ACTOR SIX. Farmer's Liberation Army.

ACTOR NINE. Guardian Knights of Justice.

ACTOR TWO. Young and old.

ACTOR TEN. Invisible Empire of the Ku Klux Klan.

ACTOR NINE. Knights of the Ku Klux Klan.

ACTOR SIX. National Association for the Advancement of White People.

ACTOR FOUR. National Democratic Front. National Socialist Liberation Front.

ACTOR FIVE. National Socialist White People's Party.

ACTOR FOUR. National State's Rights Party.

ACTOR TWO. East and west.

ACTOR THREE. New Order Knights.

ACTOR FOUR. Posse Comitatus.

ACTOR TWO. North and south.

ACTOR TEN. Socialist Anarchist Nazi Remnant.

ACTOR SIX. Socialist Nationalist Aryan People's Party.

ACTOR FOUR. SS Action Group.

ACTOR FIVE. Teenage Commando Squad.

ACTOR SIX. United Klans of America.

ACTOR TWO. Some advocate separatism.

ACTOR NINE. White Aryan Resistance. White Knights of Liberty.

ACTOR FOUR. White Patriot Party.

ACTOR THREE. White Student Union.

ACTOR TWO. Some advocate extermination.

PASTOR ONE, PASTOR TWO, PASTOR THREE. Let us pray.

(*MUSIC STOPS.*
The PASTORS bow their heads. The CAST turns toward them, with the exception of ACTOR TWO who speaks to the audience.)

ACTOR TWO. There is one common bond for the majority of these groups. A set of religious beliefs known as the Identity Doctrine.

MUELLER. Mr. Parmenter, could you further describe what you came to know the Identity Doctrine to be?

(*As PARMENTER speaks, the BOY appears. HE wears an Aryan Nations uniform identical to Pastor One.*)

PARMENTER. Yes. It was, like I said, basically that the white people were the Israelites of the Bible. They produced a real antagonist by saying the Jews were the progeny of the devil, and that it was the responsibility of the white race to destroy the race of Jews and also to separate themselves from all other races.

BOY. We believe the Bible is the true word of Yahweh, our God, written for and about a specific people.

PASTOR ONE. The Bible is the family history of the white race, the children of Yahweh placed on the earth through the seedline of Adam.

PASTOR THREE. *Ameri* meaning heavenly.

PASTOR TWO. *Rica*, or *reich,* meaning kingdom.

PASTOR ONE. America.

BOY. Heavenly kingdom.

ACTOR TWO. In May of 1920, Henry Ford began to use a part of his automobile fortune to publish a document called *The Protocols of the Learned Elders of Zion.* These *Protocols,* which Ford claimed were issued at the first Zionist Congress in 1897, were said to be the writings of Jewish elders concerning their plan to take over the world.

(*During the following, ACTOR NINE and ACTOR TEN enter. THEY each wear long black robes, a yarmulke, and a tallith. THEY each hold a large, black book.*)

ACTOR TWO. Ford, to prove his theory of a Jewish conspiracy, had the *Protocols* printed in the *Dearborn Independent* throughout the twenties. They were then collected in book form and titled *The International Jew: The World's Foremost Problem.*

ACTOR THREE. They were distributed by every Ford dealer in America.

ACTOR TEN. Protocol Number 11, Article 4:

ACTOR TWO. The *Protocols* depict the Jewish race as the cause of world-wide turmoil.

ACTOR TEN. "The goyim are a flock of sheep and we are their wolves. And you know what happens when the wolves get hold of the flock."

ACTOR THREE. The Jews are held responsible for communism, trade unions, the Russian revolution, the gold standard, the murder of Christ, and finance capitalism.

ACTOR NINE. Protocol Number 8, Article 2: "We shall surround ourselves with a whole constellation of bankers, industrialists, capitalists, and the main thing – millionaires – because, in substance, everything will be settled by figures."

ACTOR THREE. It was later revealed that the *Protocols* were not written by Jews at all. The were forged by the *Dearborn Independent's* editor, William Cameron.

(*During the following, ACTOR NINE and ACTOR TEN tear the robe, yamulke and tallith from their bodies ... revealing them to be dressed as the CANDIDATES. The CANDIDATES wear the Aryan Nations uniform.*)

ACTOR NINE/CANDIDATE. Protocol Number 5, Article 11:

ACTOR TEN/CANDIDATE. "By all these means we shall so wear down the goyim that they will be compelled to offer us international power— —"

ACTOR NINE/CANDIDATE. "Of a nature that by its very position will enable us,without any violence, —"

ACTOR TEN/CANDIDATE. "Gradually to absorb all the state forces of the world and to form a Super Government."

ACTOR THREE. Though exposed and admitted to as forgery, the *Protocols* are still readily available today throughout the radical right.

ACTOR NINE/CANDIDATE. Protocol Number 15, Article 1:

ACTOR TWO. They used as a call to arms for the white race in its battle against ZOG — the Zionist Occupation Government.

ACTOR TEN/CANDIDATE. "We shall slay without mercy all who takes arms in hand to oppose our coming into our kingdom."

BOY. We believe there are literal children of Satan in the world today.

PASTOR TWO. These children are the descendants of Cain, who was born of Eve's physical seduction by Satan.

PASTOR THREE. These people are a race of Mongolian-Turkish Khazars who are known in the world today as *Jews*.

BOY. We believe that the Canaanite Jew is the natural enemy of the white race.

PASTOR ONE. This is attested to by Scripture and ALL secular history.

ACTOR SIX. William Cameron, who forged the *Protocols*, went on to found the Anglo-Saxon Federation of America in 1928, which published *Destiny* magazine – the leading racist periodical of its day.

ACTOR TWO. A California Klan member by the name of Wesley Swift was highly influenced by the magazine, and began to incorporate these theories of a Jewish conspiracy into the white supremacist movement.

ACTOR THREE. Swift founded the Church of Jesus Christ-Christian in 1946, and traveled nationwide promoting its message.

ACTOR SIX. Swift's original church in Lancaster, California, was inherited by a man named Richard Butler.

ACTOR TWO. Butler moved the church to Hayden Lake, Idaho, in the early seventies.

ACTOR THREE. Where it continues to this day.

(*LIGHTS OUTS on ACTOR TWO, ACTOR THREE and ACTOR SIX.*)

BOY. We believe that the true, literal children of the Bible are the Twelve Lost Tribes of Israel.

PASTOR ONE. Ancient Israel, following the reign of Solomon, was divided into twelve tribes named after the twelve sons of Jacob.

BOY. Jacob was the son of Abraham. He was not a Jew.

PASTOR ONE. After the exodus from Egypt, God gave each of the twelve tribes a place in the Promised Land. In 585 B.C., however, the tribes were conquered and run out of the area by the Assyrians. They then became known as the Twelve Lost Tribes of Israel.

PASTOR THREE. Although there is no further mention of these tribes in the Bible, it has been historically PROVEN that these tribes remained intact and left Assyria by crossing the Caucasus mountains.

PASTOR TWO. And the descendants of these people are known, to this day, as *Caucasians.*

PASTOR ONE. The tribe of Ephraim became Great Britain.

BOY. The tribe of Benjamin became Iceland.

PASTOR TWO. The tribe of Gad became Italy.

BOY. The tribe of Reuben became Holland.

PASTOR TWO. The tribes of Zebulun and Judah became France and Germany.

PASTOR THREE. The tribes of Issachar and Naphtali became Finland and Norway.

BOY. The tribes of Dan and Asher became Denmark and Sweden.

PASTOR ONE. And the tribe of Manasseh moved across the Atlantic on the *Mayflower* and were given SACRED DOCUMENTS called the Declaration of Independence, the Constitution and the Bill of Rights.

PASTOR THREE. *Ameri* meaning heavenly.

PASTOR TWO. *Rica,* or *reich,* meaning kingdom.

BOY. This tribe became known as the United States of America.

PASTOR ONE. Heavenly kingdom.

(*The PASTORS, the CANDIDATES and the BOY all give a Nazi salute.*
MUSIC: "See That My Grave is Kept Clean" by Bob Dylan, verse three.*
LIGHTS shift. The cemetery, as before.
The three WOMEN enter with notepads, shining FLASHLIGHTS, as before.)

ACTOR TWO.	ACTOR FOUR.	ACTOR SIX.
Charles Lee Austin.	Chad W. Singer	Michael Harris.

---

* See Production Note on page 165.

ACTOR TWO	ACTOR FOUR.	ACTOR SIX.
William Alan Rogers.	Bruce William Fry.	Monte Ross Sharpe.
Scott Adam Walker.	Edgar Lynn Williams.	Richard Black.
Roger L. Morton.	Earnest James Hunter.	Steve J. Lewis.
Michael Schmidt	Dana Swift Nelson	Bette Wilder.
Scott William Allgood.	Andrew Smith.	Eric Hartman
David Zimmerman.	Wyatt Hunter.	Gladys Engstrom.
Mark Edward Raymond	Molley Bradley.	Mathew Mark Samuels.
Ann Payne.	Robert Sterling.	Tom D. Benjamin.
Patrick LaRouche.	Dan White.	Pat Stone.

(*ACTOR FOUR and ACTOR SIX sit and consider their lists.*
ACTOR TWO turns and speaks to the audience.
MUSIC FADES.)

ACTOR TWO. A letter arrives one day. My husband opens it. "The burial of the time capsule will take place in your yard this Sunday. Be prepared to place items of great importance in the capsule, which will be opened after the coming Armageddon, as foretold in the book of Revelations by the prophet John."

Our yard is a mess. There will be cameras and Koppel and my snapdragons won't stand a chance. Women with hair of steel will pummel me with questions and make my dog do tricks he's forgotten. They're trying to make me an event.

My husband begins filling a huge cardboard box with post-apocalyptic belongings. We'll want some magazines, he says. Some playing cards. Beef jerky. I begin to question the value of a Coleman stove in the face of the Four Horsemen and the Seven-Headed Beasts rising up out of the sea. He packs extra socks. I walk out and look at the sky.

Tell us: Why were you chosen and where did the letter come from and what is your religion and do you read our paper and will you sell our breath mints and can you talk with the President and here's another telegram from Israel and Jericho and Idaho and can we get a shot of you with your husband and child and can we get a shot of you cooking and cleaning and breast-feeding and can you sign this for my daughter her name's Edward?

The cardboard box is overflowing with my husband's essentials. Credit cards and condoms and fire insurance are sprouting out of the top.

The yard is overflowing with lipstick and technology. My husband puts the box on a dolly and wheels it out through the cheering crowd. I stand in the doorway, holding my baby.

A man in a silk suit, with a huge forehead and ill-fitting teeth, walks through the crowd in my direction. He carries a shiny, stainless steel tube. Three feet long. His forehead is in my face. The cameras are rolling. He is smiling at my baby. The flashes are flashing. He is smiling at my baby. I yell to my husband. He is smiling at my baby. As I tighten my grip, I am holding only myself. Sleeping amid the chaos, my baby is carried away. I see the capsule opened. A prayer is spoken. I see the capsule close around his body. A shaft in the center of the yard is unveiled. The capsule goes in the earth as the reporters go on the air. The crowd explodes into confetti. And I saw an angel come down from heaven. My husband stands in the driveway, wrapping up a movie deal. And the angel laid hold on the Serpent, which is the Devil. My neighbors are giving exclusives. And the Serpent was cast into the bottomless pit and a seal was set upon him that he should deceive the nations no more.

The man with the huge forehead drives away. I grab at the earth. Alpha and Omega. I grab at the air. The first and the last. I stand in my yard. I am holding only myself.

(MUSIC: "See That My Grave is Kept Clean" by
  Bob Dylan, * *verse five.*
LIGHTS shift as the WOMEN exit the cemetery.
  LIGHTS reveal LAKE at the center bench.
MUSIC FADES.)

ROBINSON. The government calls Mr. Peter Lake.

ACTOR NINE. A California writer and filmmaker who had infiltrated the Aryan Nations church in 1983, around the time The Order was being formed. Lake took numerous video tapes of Order activities, and later wrote an article for *The Rebel*, a short-lived magazine published by Larry Flynt.

ROBINSON. Mr. Lake, are you familiar with a book entitled *The Turner Diaries*?

LAKE. Yes.

ROBINSON. *(Handing him a copy of the book.)* Would you open that up and tell us if you recognize the contents?

LAKE. Yes, I do.

ROBINSON. Now, did there come a time when you had a discussion with the defendant Frank Silva about *The Turner Diaries?*

LAKE. Yes. He said: "You should read it, partner. It's all there. Everything's that's going to happen is in *The Turner Diaries.*"

---

* See Production Note on page 165.

ROBINSON. Did you read *The Turner Diaries?*

LAKE. I didn't read *The Turner Diaries* then. I couldn't find a copy. Everybody was telling me to read it and I couldn't find a copy to read.

ROBINSON. Did you finally get to read it?

LAKE. Yes, I did.

ROBINSON. Who is listed as the purported author of *The Turner Diaries?*

LAKE. Andrew MacDonald.

ROBINSON. Do you know, in fact, who *is* the author?

LAKE. William Pierce.

ROBINSON. Who is William Pierce?

HALPRIN. Your Honor, I'll object. He's laid no foundation.

VOICE OF COURT/ACTOR FIVE. Lay a foundation, please.

ROBINSON. How do you know that William Pierce wrote *The Turner Diaries?*

LAKE. (*Showing book to audience.*) His copyright is on the inside page.

ROBINSON. Do you know who William Pierce is?

LAKE. Yes, he is head of a group called the National Alliance, based in Washington, D.C., said to be an ultra right-wing —

HALPRIN. I will object to that, "said to be," and ask that it be stricken.

VOICE OF COURT/ACTOR FIVE. So ordered.

ROBINSON. What was your *understanding* of the National Alliance?

LAKE. The National Alliance is a far right-wing organization –

HALPRIN. I will object to that. There is *no foundation.*

VOICE OF COURT/ACTOR FIVE. Overruled. This is a statement.

ROBINSON. Do you know where it is headquartered?

LAKE. (*To Halprin.*) In Washington, D.C.

ROBINSON. This book, *The Turner Diaries*, does it purport to be a book of fiction or non-fiction?

(*As LAKE speaks, LIGHTS rise slowly on MATHEWS. HE wears camouflaged pants and a t-shirt. HE removes his glasses. HE begins to clean a weapon.*)

LAKE. It is fiction. In 1991, *The Turner Diaries* describes the United States as being under the control of oppressive elements – Jewish controlled, black controlled elements – who have corrupted the   government and virtually enslaved the citizens of the United States. A counter-revolutionary, super-secret group called The Order attempts, through various means of assassination, counterfeiting, revolutionary violence, to overthrow the government of the United States, beginning on the West Coast.

(ZILLAH CRAIG enters with the BOY. The BOY sits next to MATHEWS. ZILLAH stands behind them.)

LAKE. During an apocalyptic moment called "The Day of the Rope," they hang media people, judges, senators, anyone in authority is killed.

MATHEWS. *(To the Boy.)* There is a small, cohesive group within this nation working day and night to make this happen. These are the same people that Henry Ford and Charles Lindbergh tried to warn us about. Had we been more vigilant, our future would not be so dark.

LAKE. And gradually The Order takes over the country.

(MATHEWS shows the BOY the pendant which ZILLAH is holding.)

MATHEWS. Do not ever underestimate the power of this pendant.

ZILLAH. The silver is symbolic of integrity, the shield is our honor, the cross represents our faith.

MATHEWS. The battle axe means that only from the spilling of blood will the future of our people be secured.

(ZILLAH puts the pendant around MATHEWS' neck.)

LAKE. The hero, Earl Turner, finally dies in a nuclear attack on the Pentagon. He is seen as a hero, a martyr.

MATHEWS. (*Holding the Boy's face in his hands.*) A great struggle is just ahead of us, and many trials and tribulations are awaiting us.

LAKE. And the implication is that the movement will then spread beyond the shores of the United States to include the whole world.

(*MATHEWS gives the BOY the weapon he was cleaning.*)

ZILLAH. But as long as one member of The Order is alive, The Order lives.

(*The BOY takes the gun and exits. MATHEWS and ZILLAH follow him off, arm in arm.*)

VOICE OF COURT/ACTOR FIVE. (*On mike.*) Mr. Halprin.

HALPRIN. Did any of these people that you met at the Aryan Nations church have relatives of mixed racial background?

LAKE. Not that I knew.

HALPRIN. Do you think it was very likely?

LAKE. Not likely at all.

HALPRIN. What do you think of the chances that someone would have *Filipino grandchildren* and a *Filipino daughter-in-law* —

ROBINSON. (*Overlapping.*) Objection. Calling for speculation.

VOICE OF COURT/ACTOR FIVE. I think Mr. Halprin is entitled to ask this question before you interrupt.

ROBINSON. Sorry.

VOICE OF COURT/ACTOR FIVE. After he asks his question, if you have an objection you may certainly make it.

HALPRIN. What do you think the chances are that one who would have a *Filipino* daughter-in-law and *Filipino* grandchildren would be a member of this group?

ROBINSON. Objection. Calling for speculation.

VOICE OF COURT/ACTOR FIVE. Why don't you ask him if he *saw them?*

HALPRIN. (*Pause.*) Did you see any such people?

LAKE. No.

HALPRIN. And what did the sign say at the front entrance?

LAKE. "WHITES ONLY."

HALPRIN. No further questions.

(*LIGHTS shift to BERG at the radio console.*)

BERG. 861-TALK. 861-8255. You're on the air.

ACTOR FIVE. (*In shaft of LIGHT.*) I have got a few things I would like to say about Jewish people. I, myself, am a Christian, okay. But Alan

— some of the best people I have ever known in my life are Jewish people. The have been *close friends,* they're *warm,* —

BERG. I don't think that means anything connected with this argument.

ACTOR FIVE. Yeah, well, it's important that that be *said* —

BERG. I don't think it is important. I think it is nonsensical, stroking, almost *anti-Semitic* —

ACTOR FIVE. They're *proud,* they're *hardworking,* as businessmen they'll *clean your plow* in the free enterprise system —

BERG. Don't forget, the Jews have their own fashion of being clannish and prejudiced. It's a part of living. We cling to our own. We're afraid of difference, when difference is the way we learn more. (*Pushes a button. New caller.*)

ACTOR TEN. (*In shaft of LIGHT.*) I have not called before, but I have been so riled up and so disappointed in the kind of people that there are in the world. It really makes me sick.

BERG. Now see, when you hear voices on here, don't think these are *rare* voice. These are representatives of tens of thousands of people.

ACTOR TEN. It just shakes me up so bad that people turn their backs on the Holocaust and say it didn't happen.

BERG. "It will never happen again."

ACTOR TEN. It will never happen —

BERG. The only place I could ever see that same thing happening again is here in the United States.

BERG. (*Pushes a button. LIGHTS out on ACTOR TEN.*) The only reason I am fighting for Elliott and Farrell, if you want to call it fighting for them, is that it always scares me if we do anything to interfere with freedom of expression. It always ends up hurting the minority.

(*ANATH WHITE enters, hands BERG a slip of paper, and exits.*)

BERG. Rick Elliott has just advised us that, in fact, he's had a threat on his life based on what we have discussed here on the air. This, I think, is a valid point to bring up here. This is *not* the way to handle it. This is usually done on *me*. I'm always getting the threats on my life. This is not going to solve anything whatsoever. I don't like what Rick had to say, I don't like what Colonel Farrell had to say, but we're *discussing something* and hopefully we'll make some sense out of this thing. I am in *no way* advocating — or have I at any time in the show — violence against these people or anyone else who doesn't agree with me. To the callers out there who threatened them: You're all wet, too. (*Pushes a button. Shaft of LIGHT on LANE.*)

ACTOR TWO. Because of the negative publicity generated by the show, most of Rick Elliott's advertisers pulled out. This cost a man named David Lane his job at the newspaper.

LANE. I was run out of Denver by the Jews media.

ACTOR TWO. Lane would lie awake at night, listening to the Berg show.

ACTOR FOUR. (*In shaft of LIGHT.*) You had a rough day today.

BERG. I didn't have a rough day.

ACTOR FOUR. Yeah, well, you had a lively day.

BERG. My dear, dealing with people like this is dealing with duck soup.

ACTOR FOUR. You're going to have the John Birch society after you.

BERG. (*Laughs.*) Oh, god. (*Pushes a button. LIGHTS out on ACTOR FOUR.*)

ACTOR TWO. David Lane made tapes of Berg's conversations with members of the radical right.

ACTOR NINE. (*In shaft of LIGHT.*) While I agree with you, fundamentally, that the guests you had appeared to be bigots, I have an objection to the way you handled them.

BERG. Well, you go right ahead –

ACTOR NINE. You tend to dominate these conversations and act more like a prosecuting attorney than a moderator.

BERG. I am *challenging* the prosecutor.

LANE. He's a filthy Jew.

BERG. I am giving them the sources and they are still screaming "You're wrong, Alan, you're wrong." What kind of thinking ability is *that?* (*Pushes a button. LIGHTS out on ACTOR NINE.*)

BERG. If you challenge people's beliefs it's like pulling the rug out from under them.

ACTOR TWO. Lane played the tapes of Berg's show for the Church of Christ in LaPorte, Colorado.

ACTOR SIX. (*In shaft of LIGHT.*) Hello, Alan. How are you?

BERG. All right.

ACTOR SIX. First of all, I just want to say that you make me so mad sometimes I would like to strangle you.

ACTOR TWO. After playing the tapes, Lane spoke to the congregation.

ACTOR SIX. I had one other thing to say.

LANE. Somebody.

ACTOR SIX. Thank God for Alan Berg and the fact that you speak up like you do.

LANE. Somebody ought to shoot that guy.

(*LIGHTS shift to PARMENTER and MUELLER. A LIGHT remains on BERG as HE relaxes, off the air, at his radio console.*)

PARMENTER. We were discussing the possibility of doing a Step Five operation.

MUELLER. Meaning what?

PARMENTER. Meaning assassination.

MUELLER. What individuals were designated or singled out as targets for assassination?

PARMENTER. Henry Kissinger, David Rockefeller, the leaders of the three networks –

MUELLER. Why were the broadcast networks on such a list?

PARMENTER. It was felt the news media was one of the vehicles responsible for poisoning the minds of our people.

MUELLER. Anyone else?

PARMENTER. Morris Dees.

MUELLER. Who did you understand Morris Dees to be?

PARMENTER. Mr. Dees had some organization in Atlanta. He was monitoring white movement groups and harassing them. And he's also Jewish.

MUELLER. Anyone else?

PARMENTER. Norman Lear.

MUELLER. Who did you understand Norman Lear to be?

PARMENTER. He was a television producer.

MUELLER. Why did the group think Mr. Lear deserved to be killed?

PARMENTER. Well, he was a Jew. Plus all of his programs were thought to be anti-white, and they were thought to be attacking what we considered white moral principles.

MUELLER. Were there any other names mentioned as possible assassination targets?

PARMENTER. Yes. Alan Berg.

MUELLER. Who did you understand Alan Berg to be?

PARMENTER. He was a radio talk show host in Denver, Colorado.

MUELLER. And why was he under discussion as someone who should be killed?

PARMENTER. He was – he had made some outspoken remarks or had some interviews with the white movement people. He was very belligerent toward the white movement, and he was a very belligerent individual in general.

MUELLER. Was it a premise of the group to kill anyone it thought to be a belligerent individual?

PARMENTER. No. He was mainly thought to be anti-white.

BERG. Talk radio is like Russian roulette.

PARMENTER. And he was Jewish.

BERG. When you push that button, you never know what will happen. (*Pushes a button. The LIGHT on him snaps out. Shafts of LIGHT discover ACTOR TEN and ACTOR SIX.*)

ACTOR TEN. Following the oath-taking at Robert Mathews' farm in September, members of The Order commit their first crime on October 28, 1983. Mathews, Pierce, Randy Duey and Dan Bauer drive to an adult bookstore in Spokane, Washington.

PARMENTER. We wanted to attack those things we thought were detrimental to our society. Pimps, porno stores, adult theatres, things like that.

ACTOR TEN. Mathews, Pierce and Duey enter the store. Bauer waits outside in the getaway car.

PARMENTER. Mr. Duey related a scene to me where he struck one of the clerks. He was amazed the clerk wasn't more stunned than he was. Apparently, he took the blow quite well. They tied the people up with tape and left the scene.

ACTOR TEN. The porno store robbery nets The Order $369 and ten cents.

ACTOR SIX. November, 1983. Six Order members travel to Seattle.

PARMENTER. We had intended — the trip was intended to go over there and rob an armored car. That was our intention. Maybe not specifically an armored car, but we were intending to rob something.

ACTOR SIX. The six men check into one room at the Golden West motel.

PARMENTER. We surveyed different locations. A Fred Meyer store, and a K-Mart. The Fred Meyer store was voted to be the best possibility.

MUELLER. Now, while you were in Seattle, did you discuss any other illegal activities besides pulling a robbery?

PARMENTER. Yes. Mr. Bauer had brought up a bit of news that was of interest to us. That a Rothschild would be coming to the area.

MUELLER. A what?

PARMENTER. Excuse me?

MUELLER. A what would be coming to the area?

PARMENTER. A Rothschild. I can't remember his first name. He was — we understood he was to be a banker from France.

MUELLER. That would be a Baron Rothschild?

PARMENTER. Yes.

SAVAGE. Well, Mr Parmenter, do you know in fact that he was a banker?

PARMENTER. I think he was a banker, yes.

SAVAGE. Well, he might have been a banker, might not have been a banker, correct?

PARMENTER. I said I think he's a banker.

SAVAGE. I see. What was the meeting all about that he was coming to?

PARMENTER. I'm not sure. I don't recall.

SAVAGE. Well, who was he talking to?

PARMENTER. The best I can recollect is that it was a meeting of — some kind of Jewish religious type meeting.

SAVAGE. And I understand that you went to the University of Washington and you went to the library and you looked up a publication, is this correct?

PARMENTER. Mr. Bauer and I looked up in a Jewish publication and found out that he was going to have his meeting at the Four Seasons Olympic Hotel in Seattle.

MUELLER. Is that in downtown Seattle?

PARMENTER. Yes.

SAVAGE. What did the hotel look like?

PARMENTER. It was very big, it was downtown, very big, very luxurious, nice hotel.

SAVAGE. Well, can you give me any further help? A "big hotel downtown that looks nice" covers quite a few.

PARMENTER. You're talking over a year ago, more than that.

MUELLER. What happened then?

SAVAGE. Well, what did the outside look like? What *color* was it?

PARMENTER. I don't recall. A light color. I know. I think it was, anyway.

MUELLER. What happened then?

SAVAGE. How *tall* was it?

PARMENTER. I know it was several stories.

SAVAGE. Most hotels are, aren't they? How *many* stories, more or less than twenty?

PARMENTER. I don't know.

MUELLER. What happened then?

SAVAGE. Isn't this the hotel you walked around and *surveyed?*

PARMENTER. Yes.

SAVAGE. And you still don't know whether or not it was more or less than twenty stories?

PARMENTER. No, I do not.

MUELLER. Mr. Parmenter, what —

PARMENTER. You want me just to proceed?

MUELLER. Yes.

PARMENTER. We went to the Olympic Hotel. We were thinking about blowing up the reception area or wherever he was going to speak. We wanted to kill him.

MUELLER. Did you carry out the bombing plan?

PARMENTER. No, we did not.

MUELLER. Why not?

PARMENTER. We didn't have any explosives.

MUELLER. Were there further discussions concerning the plan to rob the armored car at the Fred Meyer store?

PARMENTER. Yes, there were. Dan Bauer raised an objection to it.

MUELLER. What was the objection?

PARMENTER. The objection was primarily on religious grounds. Whether we actually had the right to rob as a means of funding The Order.

MUELLER. The robbery was called off, is that correct?

PARMENTER. That's correct.

MUELLER. Did you return to Cheney?

PARMENTER. Yes, I did. Things were left kind of up in the air as to what direction The Order would take. And as to my personal affairs, I was still having trouble with my wife.

MUELLER. So, you dropped out of contact with the group for awhile?

PARMENTER. Yes.

ACTOR SIX. December, 1983. Robert Jay Mathews single-handedly robs the Innis Arden branch of the City Bank in Seattle. He leaves with $25,900.

ACTOR TEN. January, 1984. Bruce Pierce and Gary Yarbrough rob the Washington Mutual Savings Bank in Spokane. They leave with $3600.

ACTOR SIX. March, 1984. Four Order members return to the Fred Meyer store they had surveyed in November of '83. They corner George King, a guard for Continental Armed Transport Company. They put guns to King's head and remove the money from his metal cart.

ACTOR TEN. The Fred Meyer robbery nets The Order $39,465.

MUELLER. What did Mr. Duey tell you?

PARMENTER. That he participated in the carrier job at the Fred Meyer store in Seattle.

MUELLER. Did he show you anything?

PARMENTER. He showed me money that he had gotten from the robbery.

MUELLER. How much money?

PARMENTER. He said it was seven thousand dollars, his share of the proceeds.

SAVAGE. You had a job at Key Tronics. You were working a mold machine?

PARMENTER. Yes.

SAVAGE. And your rate of pay there?

PARMENTER. Three eighty-nine an hour.

SAVAGE. Then you rejoined The Order after Mr. Duey showed you seven thousand dollars that purportedly came from a Seattle robbery?

PARMENTER. Among other things, yes. I wanted to get into those activities.

SAVAGE. So, you joined for *philosophical* reasons?

PARMENTER. The same reasons I was involved in the first place.

SAVAGE. If Mr. Duey had told you in March of '84 that they had gone to Seattle and made about *five dollars apiece* in this robbery, do you think you would have rejoined?

PARMENTER. The reason I rejoined was because The Order was *doing something*. We didn't do this for personal gain.

SAVAGE. You didn't do this for personal gain?

PARMENTER. No.

SAVAGE. Did you still think that robbing people was irreligious when you rejoined the group?

PARMENTER. I think we're getting tied up in a misunderstanding here —

SAVAGE. Just a second —

PARMENTER. I did not say it was irreligious.

SAVAGE. Mr. Bauer said robbery was inappropriate on religious grounds. Isn't that what you testified to yesterday?

PARMENTER. Yes.

SAVAGE. And you agreed with him?

PARMENTER. Yes.

SAVAGE. *Now* Mr. Duey shows you seven thousand dollars and you rejoin The Order, correct?

PARMENTER. Yes.

SAVAGE. Do you *now* think that it is inappropriate to rob people on religious grounds?

PARMENTER. No.

SAVAGE. And what has happened in the meantime to *change your mind?*

PARMENTER. We had rethought the matter. It was felt that it was necessary to gain money by some means – whether it was illegitimate or not – to fund the group, to bring our cause and our goals to fruition.

SAVAGE. And when did you and Mr. Duey have this discussion?

PARMENTER. The same day.

SAVAGE. And on that day, why, you finally *realized* that religiously it was *okay* to rob people?

PARMENTER. It was thought that this robbing people was at least a minor matter when we had these ultimate, higher goals.

SAVAGE. And within four months you had made about *sixty-five thousand dollars* for yourself, hadn't you?

PARMENTER. Yes.

SAVAGE. Now, that sure beats working for Key Tronics, doesn't it?

PARMENTER. That could be a way one could take it, yes.

SAVAGE. Thank you. (*Exits.*)

ACTOR TEN. April, 1984. Seven Order members return to Seattle — and this time take separate rooms at a Motel 6. Their target is a Bon Marche department store located in the Northgate shopping mall.

ACTOR SIX. Using two vehicles, The Order pins the armored car to the Bon Marche loading dock.

ACTOR TEN. Mathews holds a sign up to the window of the armored car.

MUELLER. What did the sign say?

PARMENTER. "Get Out Or Die."

ACTOR TEN. The guards get out of the car. One of the guards looks familiar.

ACTOR SIX. It is George King, the victim of the Fred Meyer robbery. Bruce Pierce says to King:

ACTOR TEN. "You know the score, George."

ACTOR SIX. King sits on the sidewalk with the other guards. The money is loaded into one of The Order's vehicles.

ACTOR TEN. The take from the Northgate robbery is $235,000.

MUELLER. Did you receive a portion of that robbery loot for your own benefit?

PARMENTER. Yes, I did.

MUELLER. Approximately how much?

PARMENTER. Approximately $24,000.

MUELLER. What did the others receive?

PARMENTER. Around in that neighborhood.

ACTOR SIX. The Order's success emboldened them. In the coming months they would begin to successfully eliminate traitors they felt were in their midst.

ACTOR TEN. May, 1984. The murder of Walter West.

ACTOR SIX. And enemies who were still at large.

ACTOR TEN. June, 1984. The murder of Alan Berg.

ACTOR SIX. Their preparations for battle became increasingly sophisticated.

ACTOR TEN. September, 1984. The Reliance Project is formed, in which scientists are recruited to develop laser weapons for The Order. Plans to poison the water systems and disrupt the power supplies of major cities are pursued as well.

(*LIGHTS OUT on ACTOR SIX and ACTOR TEN.*)

MUELLER. Mr. Parmenter, after the money had been counted out, was there any money left over?

PARMENTER. Yes, there was.

MUELLER. Did anyone suggest what should be done with the balance?

PARMENTER. Yes. To tithe the Aryan Nations church with what was thought to be ten percent.

(*PASTOR ONE enters, wearing a bright red robe and hood, his face exposed.*)

PASTOR ONE. Psalm 149: Let the High Praise of God be in their mouth, and a two-edged sword in their hand.
MUELLER. To who?
PARMENTER. Pastor Butler.

(*SLIDE: RICHARD BUTLER*
  THE CHURCH OF JESUS CHRIST-
  CHRISTIAN, HAYDEN LAKE, IDAHO

PASTOR ONE. Not everyone who walks on two legs is human. It's not that we don't respect non-Aryans. It's just that they don't have the same status as we do. We didn't CHOOSE it. God has SAID it.

(*PASTOR TWO enters, wearing a deep blue robe and hood, his face exposed.*

SLIDE: TOM METZGER
LEADER OF W.A.R.
[WHITE ARYAN RESISTANCE])

PASTOR TWO. The melting pot theory is a myth. A myth perpetrated by the corporations to blind your eyes as they pick your pockets. W.A.R. is dedicated to the white working people. The farmers. The white poor. The capitalist right wing is dead. The Marxist left wing never was alive. The is the WHITE WING. We've got ONE WAR, the same war the SA fought in Germany — RIGHT HERE IN THE STREETS OF AMERICA.

(*PASTOR THREE enters, wearing a white robe and hood, his face exposed.*

SLIDE: THOMAS ROBB
CHAPLAIN
KNIGHTS OF THE KU KLUX KLAN)

PASTOR ONE. Faith and warfare are inseparable.
PASTOR THREE. There is a WAR IN AMERICA. And there are two camps. One camp is in Washington, D.C. — controlled by the Anti-Christ Jews.
PASTOR ONE. Candidates, come forward.

(*The BOY enters, wearing the Aryan Nations uniform. HE carries a large sword. The CANDIDATES — ACTOR THREE and ACTOR FIVE — follow him on stage. THEY take places facing PASTOR ONE.*)

PASTOR THREE. MAKE NO MISTAKE ABOUT IT. Their goal is the DESTRUCTION of our race, our faith and our people. And OUR goal is the DESTRUCTION OF THEM. There is NO MIDDLE GROUND.

PASTOR ONE. Raise your arms in salute.

(The CANDIDATES raise their arms in a Nazi salute.)

PASTOR TWO. IMMIGRATION AND ABORTION ARE DESTROYING THE ARYAN RACE.

PASTOR THREE. Why are you so shocked?

PASTOR ONE. I pledge my allegiance —

PASTOR TWO.	CANDIDATES/ ACTOR THREE, FIVE. *(Soft and urgent.)*
96 percent of the 70 MILLION abortions have been abortions of white, Aryan children. PASTOR ONE. To the law ordained by my Heavenly Father —	I pledge my allegiance —

PASTOR TWO.   CANDIDATES/
                          ACTOR THREE,
                          FIVE.
This is   To the law ordained
GENOCIDE.   by my Heavenly
                          Father —
PASTOR THREE.
Did you think this
was a GAME?

(*MUSIC: "RUBRIC" By Philip Glass* * *begins,
    softly, and builds in intensity during the
    following.*)

PASTOR ONE.
To my Aryan race
which is my nation
—

---

* See Production Note on page 165.

PASTOR THREE.

Have not all the
reading, have not
all the listening to
sermons, have not
all the world events
told you that it is US
OR THEM?
PASTOR TWO.
IT IS TIME TO
MAKE WAR BY
MAKING LOVE.

CANDIDATES/
ACTOR THREE,
FIVE.
To my Aryan race
which is my nation
—

(*As the PASTORS continue their sermons,
LIGHTS reveal MATHEWS and ZILLAH
CRAIG, upstage. ZILLAH is barefoot, her hair
down. During the following, THEY
gradually unbutton and remove each other's
shirts, kiss and embrace.*)

PASTOR TWO.
It is time for every
healthy Aryan
woman to bear
children. This is a
woman's supreme
and holy task.
PASTOR ONE.
I will not betray my
commanders or
their faith in me —

PASTOR TWO.	CANDIDATES/ ACTOR THREE, FIVE.
NO kinsman should raise his sword against ZOG until he has PLANTED HIS SEED IN THE BELLY OF A WOMAN.	I will not betray my commanders or their faith in me —

PASTOR ONE.
I will never rest
until there is
created on this
continent a
NATIONAL
STATE FOR MY
PEOPLE –
PASTOR THREE.

CANDIDATES/
ACTOR THREE,
FIVE
I will never rest
until there is
created on this
continent a
National State for
my people –

THEY WANT TO
STEAL THE
MINDS OF YOUR
CHILDREN.

PASTOR TWO.
 ALL CHILDREN
BORN ARYAN
AND HEALTHY
ARE
CONSIDERED
LEGITIMATE.
  PASTOR ONE.
This pledge I take
before God and in
sight of these my
Aryan brothers –

PASTOR THREE.

CANDIDATES/
ACTOR THREE,
FIVE.
This pledge I take
before God and in
sight of these my
Aryan brothers.

"ANY
ALLEGIANCE
WHOSE PURPOSE
IS NOT THE
INTENTION TO
WAGE WAR IS
SENSELESS AND
USELESS."
PASTOR TWO.
  EVERY CHILD
THAT AN ARYAN
MOTHER BRINGS
INTO THE
WORLD IS A
BATTLE WAGED
FOR THE
EXISTENCE OF
HER PEOPLE.
PASTOR THREE.
  "IT IS NOT
RIGHT THAT
MATTERS, BUT
VICTORY."
      PASTOR ONE. One God –
      PASTOR THREE. "HAVE NO PITY."
      CANDIDATES, PASTOR TWO, BOY. (*Full
voice.*) ONE GOD –
      PASTOR ONE. One Nation –

PASTOR THREE. "ADOPT A BRUTAL ATTITUDE."

CANDIDATES, PASTOR TWO, BOY. ONE NATION –

PASTOR THREE. "RIGHT IS ON THE SIDE OF THE STRONGEST."

PASTOR ONE. One Race.

PASTOR THREE. "BY WARDING OFF THE JEWS, I AM FIGHTING FOR THE LORD'S WORK."

CANDIDATES, PASTOR TWO, BOY. ONE RACE.

(The CANDIDATES kneel. PASTOR ONE takes the sword from the BOY and knights them on each shoulder while saying the following.)

PASTOR ONE. I lay upon you the Sword of Truth, knighting you in brotherhood for the glory of Yahweh, our God.

BOY. We believe that HATE is our law.

PASTOR ONE. Great your new comrades.

BOY. And REVENGE is our duty.

(The CANDIDATES turn and face the audience. Abrupt LIGHT shift to ACTOR NINE, standing in the audience. HE is a young man in a conservative suit.

MUSIC STOPS ABRUPTLY.
SLIDE: GREG WITHROW
PRESIDENT
THE WHITE STUDENT UNION)

ACTOR NINE. We are not right or left wing.
We are RACISTS. We are now officially
operating an underground chapter on your
campus, and over thirty chapters nationwide. The
NEXT line of leadership shall be a generation of
ruthless predators that shall make PAST Aryan
leaders and warriors PALE IN COMPARISON.
If peaceful means fail, the white youth of this
nation shall utilize EVERY METHOD AND
OPTION AVAILABLE TO THEM to neutralize
and quite possibly engage in WHOLESALE
EXTERMINATION OF ALL SUB-HUMAN,
NON-ARYAN PEOPLES FROM THE FACE OF
THE NORTH AMERICAN CONTINENT.

(LIGHTS return abruptly to the full stage.
PASTOR ONE, PASTOR TWO and PASTOR
THREE hold flaming torches.
MATHEWS and ZILLAH CRAIG, both shirtless
now, continue to kiss and embrace in
silhouette, upstage.
Brilliant red/orange LIGHT engulfs both the
stage and the theatre itself.

MUSIC: "Rubric[*] returns and begins building to
    a crescendo.)*

PASTOR ONE. MY ARYAN BROTHERS,
BEHOLD THE GLORY OF YAHWEH, OUR
GOD. AS WARRIORS FOR OUR GOD, WE
COME TO LIGHT THE HOLY CROSS OF OUR
ARYAN SAVIOR. BEHOLD THE WHITE FIRE
WHICH HAS RAGED IN THE HEARTS OF
OUR HEROES. HEROES SUCH AS JACK
LONDON, CHARLES LINDBERGH, RUDOLPH
HESS, GEORGE LINCOLN ROCKWELL AND
JOE McCARTHY. MARTYRS SUCH AS
GORDON KAHL, ADOLPH HITLER AND
ROBERT JAY MATHEWS.

PASTOR TWO. THERE IS A VIOLENCE
THAT LIBERATES AND A VIOLENCE THAT
ENSLAVES.

PASTOR THREE. DO THE WORK WHICH IS
REQUIRED OF YOU IN THIS SEASON –

PASTOR TWO. THERE IS A VIOLENCE
THAT IS MORAL –

PASTOR THREE. PREPARE FOR THE WORK
AHEAD.

PASTOR TWO. AND A VIOLENCE THAT IS
IMMORAL.

PASTOR ONE. OUR LIGHT CAME FROM
THE CROSS –

---

[*] See Production Note on page 165.

PASTOR THREE. KNOW THAT THE HOUR OF THE HARVEST COMES.

PASTOR ONE. AND SHALL RETURN TO THE CROSS.

PASTOR THREE. IN THE RIGHT TIME, MORE THAN JUST THE MOON SHALL RISE.

(*The PASTORS cover their faces with their hoods.*)

PASTOR ONE. WHAT YOU SEE TONIGHT –

PASTOR TWO. HAIL VICTORY.

PASTOR THREE, CANDIDATES, BOY. HAIL VICTORY!

PASTOR ONE. WHAT YOU ARE EXPERIENCING TONIGHT –

PASTOR THREE. HAIL VICTORY.

PASTOR TWO, CANDIDATES, BOY. HAIL VICTORY!

PASTOR ONE. YOU WILL NEVER AGAIN FORGET.

PASTOR ONE, PASTOR TWO, PASTOR THREE, CANDIDATES, BOY. HAIL VICTORY!

(*MUSIC STOPS ABRUPTLY.*
Fast BLACKOUT.)

END OF ACT I

GOD'S COUNTRY

ACT II

Fanaticism consists in
redoubling your efforts when you have
forgotten the aim.

Santayana

(MUSIC: "Down By the Riverside"* sung by Mahalia Jackson.
House and stage LIGHTS FADE to black.
LIGHTS rise on two men sitting in rocking chairs: MISTER SMITH and MISTER JONES. A STUDENT is setting up a tape recorder between them.
SONG FADES.)

JONES. These are not stories. These are researched conjectures. Is that hooked up, yet?

STUDENT. Not yet.

JONES. That was Mahalia Jackson.

SMITH. Outside?

JONES. No.

SMITH. I didn't see anyone. Were we followed?

JONES. That song. "Down By the Riverside." Mahalia Jackson, wasn't it?

STUDENT. Yes. I think I'm ready here.

JONES. Even before I was licensed as a conspiratologist, I had —

SMITH. Before we met at the gun show?

---

* See Production Note on page 165.

JONES. Yes. Even before I —

STUDENT. Licensed by whom?

SMITH. (*Pronounced "You Cock."*) U.C.O.C.C.

STUDENT. Pardon?

JONES. The United Coalition of Concerned Conspiratologists.

SMITH. We meet yearly at a secret location in an unspecified city.

STUDENT. I see.

SMITH. Lovely group. Even the Texans.

JONES. As I said, even before my licensing — (*Looks at tape player.*) Are you getting this?

STUDENT. Yes.

JONES. Even before that, I had uncovered the Jackson Conspiracy.

STUDENT. The J—

JONES. Look beyond your nose. Mahalia Jackson. Michael Jackson. Reggie Jackson. Jesse Jackson. Do you — I think you do — see a pattern? Subversion of traditional values. Insidious role models promoting androgency, affirmative action, and the displacement of the Baby Ruth as America's candy bar. Jack. French derivation:

SMITH. *Jacques.*

JONES. Meaning:

SMITH. *The Supplanter.*

JONES. Jackson.

JONES and SMITH. *Son of Jack.*

JONES. The Supplanter of our cherished rhythms, fashions and public offices. A burgeoning JACKSONIFICATION is sweeping this country and –

(*Sudden BLACKOUT.*)

JONES. What was that?
STUDENT. I think the power's out.
JONES. You see.
SMITH. They hate that one.

(*LIGHTS return abruptly.*)

JONES. Next question.
SMITH. We're used to it.
STUDENT. All right. First of all. I need to ask if Mister Jones and Mister Smith are your real names?
JONES and SMITH. (*To the tape player.*) Yes.

(*JONES and SMITH immediately look at the STUDENT and shake their heads "No."*)

STUDENT. All right. I have several questions about –
SMITH. (*Suddenly.*) Who *are* you?
STUDENT. Who am –
SMITH. Do we *know* her? Do we know where she's *been?* (*Turns off tape player.*) Are there

people in the bushes? Do you hear a high-pitched tone? Have the guards been alerted?

JONES. (*To Student, calmly.*) Show him your tag.

(*The STUDENT shows SMITH her clip-on identification tag.*)

JONES. There.

SMITH. Sorry. I'm thrilled you're here.

JONES. Yes.

SMITH. Go on.

SMITH. All right. There has been a preponderance —

JONES. (*Efficiently to Smith, who nods.*) A bunch.

SMITH. — Of material which suggests a conspiracy surrounding the J.F.K. assassination.

SMITH. Is she kidding? Are you kidding?

JONES. Are they still beating that horse?

STUDENT. You feel the answers have been found?

JONES. Without question.

SMITH. Anne Frank.

STUDENT. Anne Frank?

JONES. Without question.

SMITH. As you know, Anne Frank's diary is a forgery.

STUDENT. I didn't know that.

JONES. Get up earlier.

SMITH. Handwriting analysis has determined that the true author was not a young Jewish girl named Anne Frank, but a hot-blooded Greek named Aristotle Onassis, who manufactured the Holocaust Myth to gain the support of the Rockefellers, who years later conspired – with Onassis, Castro and L.B.J. – to eliminate Kennedy. Johnson got the White House. Castro got revenge. And Onassis got the girl.

(*Sudden BLACKOUT.*)

SMITH. You see.
JONES. The first reaction to truth is hatred.

(*LIGHTS return abruptly.*)

STUDENT. I'm sorry, but with all due respect, that theory sounds rather preposterous –
JONES. (*Efficiently to SMITH, who nods.*) Nuts.
STUDENT. – In the context of known facts.
JONES. There is no creed so false but faith can make it true.
SMITH. (*To JONES.*) Eight eight.
JONES. (*To SMITH.*) Eight eight. (*To STUDENT.*) Next question.
STUDENT. All right. The followers of Lyndon LaRouche have made some surprising political strides. Don't you agree that the rationale

for some of their bizarre claims seems
perfunctory —

JONES. (*Efficiently to SMITH, who nods.*)
Shallow.

STUDENT. — At best?

SMITH. Which claims?

STUDENT. The international drug trade is
financed by Jewish bankers and implemented by
the British royal family, who also ordered the
execution of Abraham Lincoln.

JONES. That's a start.

SMITH. Tip of the iceberg.

STUDENT. Going on. The B'nai B'rith
organization regularly kidnaps children for the
purpose of conducting ancient Jewish temple
rituals.

SMITH. And worse.

JONES. They're also behind the "Have a Nice
Day" greeting, which is *code* for "Track Down An
Aryan and Kill Him."

SMITH. Eight eight.

JONES. Eight eight.

STUDENT. All AIDS carriers should be
registered with the police for the purpose of
possible internment.

JONES. It Darwinism.

SMITH. It's a divinely-inspired disease.

STUDENT. Mankind's only true hope for the
future is to colonize Mars before the coming
nuclear Armageddon.

JONES. Accurate, but short-sighted.

SMITH. The Trilateralists and the International Banking Cartel have inspired each and every war of our generation.

JONES. They planned the attack on Pearl Harbor, the Tet offensive, and the mining of the Persian Gulf.

SMITH. So that through global strife, an illegal Zionistic organization like the United Nations. —

JONES. Run by David Rockefeller —

SMITH. Will use the Dear Abby column —

JONES. The Pee Wee Herman show —

SMITH. And that Budweiser dog with the black mark of Satan —

JONES. To destroy our race —

SMITH. And overrun the world!

(*Sudden BLACKOUT — then LIGHTS come immediately back up. SMITH and JONES walk toward the audience and stare at them.*)

SMITH. Do not be amused. These are not stories.

JONES. These things exist.

SMITH. Beware the ridiculous. It will one day rule you.

JONES. Eight eight.

SMITH. Eight eight.

(*SMITH and JONES snap their fingers. LIGHTS shift.*)

MUSIC: "Armagideon Time"* by the Clash.
Simultaneously, ACTOR FIVE, ACTOR SEVEN,
    ACTOR NINE and ACTOR TEN rush
    onstage. THEY wear dark denim clothes and
    ski masks on their heads – not covering their
    faces. THEY carry weapons. ACTOR NINE
    carries a stopwatch, as well.
SMITH and JONES exit, carrying the tape player
    with them. The STUDENT, as well as the
    rocking chairs, are carried out by MEN also
    dressed in dark clothes and ski masks.)

ACTOR TEN. July, 1984. Twelve Order
members gather for a morning prayer at the Motel
8 in Santa Rosa, California. They have recruited
as members two men who work for the Brink's
company in San Francisco.

ACTOR FIVE. These men agree to provide
The Order with inside information on the best
armored car routes to rob.

ACTOR TEN. The information points to an
armored car bound for Ukiah, California.

(During the following, ACTOR FIVE, ACTOR
    SEVEN and ACTOR TEN pass five large
    duffel bags of money, in a brigade, from one to
    another – until the bags are passed to a point

---

* See Production Note on page 165

*offstage. ACTOR NINE monitors a stopwatch
and lists the elapsed time.
MUSIC continues, under.)*

ACTOR SEVEN.
As the car slows,
going up a steep
grade on Route 101,
members of The
Order, using two
trucks, force the
armored car to the
side of the road.

ACTOR NINE.
Ten seconds.

Bill Soderquist
holds a sign up to
the window of the
car.

Fifteen seconds.

ACTOR FIVE.   Twenty seconds.
"Get Out Or Die."   Twenty-five
                          seconds.

ACTOR TEN.   Thirty seconds.
With military   Thirty-five
precision, money is   seconds.
removed from the
Brinks truck.

ACTOR SEVEN.
Richard Scutari
monitors police
radios and shouts
out the elapsed time
to the other men.

ACTOR TEN.
The only
complication is a
female guard who
refuses to come out
of the armored car.

ACTOR FIVE.
Randy Evans fires
a shotgun blast into
the rear
compartment where
she is hiding.

ACTOR SEVEN.
He later expresses
amazement that she
was not killed.

Forty seconds.
Forty-five seconds.

Fifty seconds.
Fifty-five seconds.

One minute.

Minute-five
seconds.
Minute-ten
seconds.
Minute-fifteen
seconds.
Minute-twenty
seconds.
Minute-twenty-five
seconds.

ACTOR TEN.   Minute and a half.
The robbers drive to
a prearranged
area, switch
automobiles, and
transport the money
to a house in Boise,
Idaho.

(*The bags have all been passed. The MEN face the
    audience.*)

ACTOR SEVEN. The take from the Ukiah
robbery is 3.6 million dollars, cash.

ACTOR TEN. All Order members receive a
six month salary of ten thousand dollars, and
participants in the robbery receive a bonus of
thirty thousand dollars.

ACTOR FIVE. Significant portions of the
money are sent to Robert Miles and his Mountain
Church in Michigan.

ACTOR SEVEN. Glenn Miller and his White
Party in North Carolina.

ACTOR NINE. Louis Beam, Identity preacher
and Texas Klan leader.

ACTOR TEN. And, naturally, William
Pierce — director of the National Alliance and
author of *The Turner Diaries*.

ACTOR FIVE. In ten months The Order had carried out the most successful crime spree in United States history.

(*LIGHTS shift as the WOMEN's voices are heard from offstage, on mike.*
The FATHER enters.)

VOICE OF ACTOR TWO.	VOICE OF ACTOR FOUR.	VOICE OF ACTOR SIX.
Charles Lee Austin.	Chad W. Singer.	Michael Harris.
VOICE OF ACTOR TWO.	VOICE OF ACTOR FOUR.	VOICE OF ACTOR SIX.
William Alan Rogers.	Bruce William Fry.	Monte Ross Sharpe.
Scott Adam Walker.	Edgar Lynn Williams.	Richard Black.
Roger L. Morton.	Earnest James Hunter.	Steve J. Lewis.
Michael Schmidt.	Dana Swift Nelson.	Bette Wilder.
Lyle Dean Nash.	William Lee Rose.	Patrick Deberio.
Floyd Shaw.	Scott McEveland.	Richard O'Connor.
Billie Salisbury.	Keith Alan Merwin.	Richard Jennings.
Scott William Allgood ...	Andrew Smith ...	Eric Hartman ...

(*The WOMEN's voices fade as the FATHER speaks to the audience.*
MUSIC OUT.)

FATHER. My wife and I fought over what to name our son. It became — the pressure of it became so real, so crucial, that we thought of nothing else. We viewed it as this stamp. This mark. Wear this, it's your name. And if you have a good name, you'll be fine. It will protect you. It will remind you of our good intentions. Remember, we love you enough to have put our marriage in jeopardy to arrive at your name. Never forget that.

Other things were less crucial. There were things I said to my son as he grew into manhood. You want your laundry fast, take it to that Chink on the corner. When you go to buy that car, don't let 'em try to Jew you down. I don't want you to take any shit from that man you work for. You're not his nigger. I did not view these things as a mark on him. They were just a necessary evil of living in a hard world. My son had his name. He would be fine. Now he's putting things in his basement.

He didn't shave his head and snort glue. He didn't stand on a street corner and use fear to hand out hope. He smiled when he shook my hand and he never missed a Father's Day. Now he's putting things in his basement.

He got a good job. Married a lovely woman. Coached Little League baseball. I did not teach him to hate. I did not teach him to be violent. I was just realistic. I just told him the way things *were*.

This morning I went to his house to borrow his mower. Had it in the basement all winter, dad. Haven't brought it up, yet. You'll see it down there. In the basement, where I had never been, were the all things my son had learned from me. There were weapons. There were explosives. There were maps outlining a proposed White Homeland. There were newspapers: *The Spotlight, The Thunderbolt, The Torch, The Way, The Aryan Nations Newsletter*. There was a picture of Adolph Hitler. And beside it, also in a place of honor, was a picture of me.

There were things I said to my son. And now he has mastered the things I only boasted of. He has a good name. And now he is putting things in his basement.

(*MUSIC: "White Power" by Skrewdriver,* * very loud.
The FATHER exits.
The SKINHEAD comes through the audience carrying two lengths of two-by-fours, which HE throws to the ground. HE removes a hammer from his pants and throws it to the*

---

* **See Production Note on page 165.**

*ground, as well. The SKINHEAD wears old
boots, torn jeans, torn leather jacket inscribed
with the words "White Power," and a black
stocking cap with a swastika crudely spray-
painted on it. The SKINHEAD points to a spot
on the floor. Nothing happens. HE glares as
the light booth. HE points again, more
adamantly. A shaft of LIGHT hits the spot
where HE pointed. HE smiles. HE points at
someone offstage. HE points to the spot on the
floor again.*

ACTOR NINE, *dressed in the conservative suit
we saw him in at the end of Act I , enters and
stands at the spot on the floor. HIS jacket and
tie are gone, his face, neck and shirt are
bloodied, and HE is barefoot. HIS hands are
bound together with rope and tape. The
SKINHEAD puts his face very near ACTOR
NINE and smiles. The SKINHEAD circles
ACTOR NINE, then leaps into the air and
brings the MUSIC to an ABRUPT STOP. HE
speaks in a fury.)*

SKINHEAD. This is OI. This music. We call
it OI. O-I, O-I, O-I. Jump cut me. Jump cut me. OI
is not punk rock. OI is not hardcore or heavy
metal. OI is Warrior music. The System has
tried to steal it to play in their elevators. The
System has tried to destroy it because it is a threat
to their tyranny. Both attempts have failed. Jump
cut me. Don't let the left hand know. Don't let the

left hand know. OI is the music of the White Warrior. Our minds are clear. Our fists are strong. Our heads are shaved for battle. (*To Actor Nine.*) TALK.

ACTOR NINE. June, 1987. White Student Union leader Greg Withrow places a phone call to his racist mentor, Tom Metzger. Withrow tells Metzger that he (quote) does not want to hate anymore (unquote). That for the first time in his life he has loved someone, a woman named Sylvia, and that in doing so he has begun to feel compassion for others. Withrow resigns as the Union's leader. He tells a reporter he has plans to write a book denouncing the white racist movement and exposing many of its crimes and conspiracies.

SKINHEAD. Skinheads of America, like the dynamic Skinheads of Europe, are working class Aryan youth. We believe in hard work. We believe that Motherhood is the most noble position to which any white woman can aspire. We believe that a family with a dominant male and a proud female is the only way to insure proper reproduction of our race. Eight eight, we say. Eight eight. Don't let the left hand know. We are at WAR with the System: the traitors, the cowards, the mud people, the apathetic, the limp-wristed queers. THIS BATTLE WILL RECEIVE OUR FULL ATTENTION. (*The SKINHEAD begins nailing the boards together in the shape of a cross.*

*His pounding punctuates ACTOR NINE's
following sentences.*)

ACTOR NINE. Despondent and fearful after
denouncing racism, Withrow attempts suicide
twice during the month of June. On July 4th, 1987,
three of Withrow's former recruits enter his
apartment in Sacramento. They club him with
baseball bats and steal the manuscript he has been
writing.

SKINHEAD. (*Having completed the
pounding.*) We are the heirs to the Revolution.
The parasitic pacifists have leeched off our land
for far too long. Our future has been bargained.
Our future has been sucked through the status quo
and left to rot on the headlines of the Capitalist
West and the bread lines of the Communist East.
Jump cut me. A *white* woman, – panhandles to
feed her baby, and Reagan sleeps soundly. And
Reagan sleeps soundly. Eight eight, we cry.
EIGHT EIGHT.

ACTOR NINE. August, 1987. Greg Withrow
leaves his Sacramento apartment. Six members
of his former group grab him, throw him in a
pickup and drive him to a vacant lot.

(*The SKINHEAD lifts the wooden cross and
carries it to behind ACTOR NINE, where HE
stands it upright.*)

SKINHEAD. Deep in the heart of the white youth is a brutal logic. This logic will leave our enemies nowhere to run.

ACTOR NINE. A six-foot long board is removed from the back of the truck.

SKINHEAD. This logic is the weapon of the white youth.

ACTOR NINE. After being brutally beaten, Withrow is strapped to the board.

SKINHEAD. It is morally invincible.

ACTOR NINE. Nails are driven through his hands.

SKINHEAD. It is ordained.

ACTOR NINE. And his throat is cut open with a razor.

SKINHEAD. Eight, eight, we cry. The eighth letter in our language: the letter "H."

ACTOR NINE. Withrow is left for dead in the vacant lot.

SKINHEAD. The letter "H," we cry: Eight. Eight. HEIL HITLER.

ACTOR NINE. He stumbles through the streets, still nailed to the board, unable to solicit help. After numerous white couples refuse to assist him, two men – a black and an Hispanic – come to his aid.

SKINHEAD. Don't let the left hand. Don't let the left hand. What the WHITE hand. What the WHITE hand is doing.

ACTOR NINE. The Sacramento County Sheriff has no suspects because Withrow is afraid to name his attackers.

SKINHEAD. Our music is OI.

ACTOR NINE. Said Withrow:

SKINHEAD. Our fists are strong.

ACTOR NINE. "They want me dead because of the things I know."

SKINHEAD. Our heads are shaved for battle. (*Thrusts the cross high in the air.*)

(*MUSIC: "Help Save the Youth of America" by*
    Billy Bragg [*] *, beginning with the verse which*
    follows the instrumental break.
BLACKOUT.
LIGHTS rise on PARMENTER at the center
    bench. SAVAGE approaches him.
MUSIC fades.)

SAVAGE. Mr. Parmenter, did you get an insurance policy in April of '84 because you were a member of The Order's inner circle?

PARMENTER. No, I was *not* a member of the inner circle.

SAVAGE. Well, when did you become a member?

PARMENTER. Right after the Ukiah robbery.

---

[*] See Production Note on page 165.

SAVAGE. But you were a member of the inner circle in April, were you not? That's one of the reasons you got the insurance.

WARD. Objection, Your Honor. The witness never said that.

VOICE OF COURT/ACTOR EIGHT. You can answer the question now.

PARMENTER. Can I explain it, Your Honor?

VOICE OF COURT/ACTOR EIGHT. Sure.

PARMENTER. I did *not* say I was a member of the inner circle. What I *said* was the members of the inner circle had gotten life insurance. I never included myself in it.

SAVAGE. Let me read this to you. Question: "Who was involved in getting life insurance policies?" Answer by you: "Mr. Duey, Mr. Pierce, Mr. Mathews and myself."

WARD. Objection, Your Honor. That doesn't say anything about —

VOICE OF COURT/ACTOR EIGHT. Let him finish the question.

WARD. That's not responsive to —

VOICE OF COURT/ACTOR EIGHT. *Sit down.*

SAVAGE. Question: "Those were members of the inner circle, weren't they?" Answer by you: "Yes, they were."

PARMENTER. That was obviously a slip-up because —

SAVAGE. Do you want to retract the answer you gave yesterday under oath?

PARMENTER. When I responded to that question, I was not –

SAVAGE. I'm sorry. I don't meant to be rude, but the question before you is do you want to retract the answer you gave yesterday under oath?

PARMENTER. I would like to clarify it.

SAVAGE. Well, go ahead. Clarify it.

PARMENTER. I did not mean to include myself.

SAVAGE. Even though you *said* yourself?

PARMENTER. I did say that, yes.

SAVAGE. You were a *leader of The Order,* is that correct?

PARMENTER. I had leadership responsibilities, yes.

RUARK. (*Enters.*) Mr. Parmenter, you've had multiple opportunities to go over your story before coming here, is this correct?

PARMENTER. I wouldn't call it a story. I would call it testimony.

RUARK. Early on in your testimony, you characterized yourself as *unstable*, is that true?

PARMENTER. That's correct.

RUARK. Would you say that still pertains to you?

PARMENTER. No, I would not.

RUARK. Since when?

PARMENTER. I would say since the time of my arrest.

HALPRIN. (*Enters.*) You said you've read the Bible several times since your DRAMATIC PRISON CONVERSION?

WARD. Objection.

HALPRIN. Excuse me. Since your conversion in jail. Is that true?

PARMENTER. That's correct.

HALPRIN. Cover to cover?

PARMENTER. Most of it.

SAVAGE. And now you've changed your beliefs, correct?

PARMENTER. Well, for one thing —

SAVAGE. Is that correct, you've changed your beliefs?

PARMENTER. Yes.

RUARK. Much of the testimony you have given here is based upon what Bob Mathews told you, isn't that correct?

PARMENTER. Some of it is, yes.

RUARK. Mr. Mathews is not going to be here to testify, is he?

PARMENTER. That's correct.

SAVAGE. And, indeed, you were candid enough to tell the jury yesterday that it would be common sense for one to *say* that he changed his beliefs in order to affect the sentencing, correct?

RUARK. And we're going to have to rely upon you as to the accuracy of what you *say* Mr. Mathews said, isn't that correct?

SAVAGE. Isn't that what you said yesterday?

PARMENTER. Yes, it is.

HALPRIN. Mr. Parmenter, you suggested earlier that one of the reasons Mr. West was killed was because he had been drinking and beating his wife?

PARMENTER. That's what I heard, yes.

HALPRIN. Did that make you feel nervous or concerned at all about *your* personal safety?

PARMENTER. No, it did not.

HALPRIN. Even though you have testified yourself that you also were a heavy drinker?

PARMENTER. That's true.

HALPRIN. And even though you have had a lot of strange situations with your own wife, isn't that true?

WARD. Your Honor, that is a *very* improper question on the part of Mr. Halprin —

HALPRIN. I will rephrase it, if you like.

VOICE OF COURT/ACTOR EIGHT. He is rephrasing the question.

HALPRIN. Would it surprise you to know that members of The Order were under the impression that you regularly beat your wife?

PARMENTER. That would *definitely* surprise me, yes.

HALPRIN. Okay —

WARD. Is he asking now *when he stopped beating his wife?!*

HALPRIN. That was my next question.

WARD. *Objection*, Your Honor. I object to his next question.

VOICE OF COURT/ACTOR EIGHT. Thank you. Next question, please.

SAVAGE. Since you joined The Order you continually lied to people, sometimes under oath, pretending to be a person you were not, didn't you?

PARMENTER. Yes, we *all* did.

SAVAGE. And you were believed, were you not?

PARMENTER. Most of the time we were, yes.

SAVAGE. Well, *you* were. I'm talking about *you*.

PARMENTER. I had different aliases, yes.

RUARK. One of the provisions of your plea agreement required you to take a polygraph?

PARMENTER. Yes.

RUARK. A lie detector, correct?

PARMENTER. Yes.

RUARK. And you did take a polygraph, did you not?

PARMENTER. I did.

RUARK. And you *failed* that polygraph and were required to take another one, weren't you?

PARMENTER. Yes, I was.

HALPRIN. What *is* an Aryan?

PARMENTER. White person.

HALPRIN. Any old white person?

PARMENTER. *Yeah.*

HALPRIN. What about me? Do I look white to you?

WARD. *Objection.*

VOICE OF COURT/ACTOR EIGHT. *Next question.*

RUARK. You've admitted you'll *lie* to protect your own self-interest, isn't that correct?

HALPRIN. Was it your hope at some point that you could eliminate *all* Jews?

PARMENTER. That was part of the doctrine, yes.

RUARK. *Isn't that correct?*

PARMENTER. There are different situations —

RUARK. Yes or no, Mr. Parmenter.

HALPRIN. Would you have been willing to kill *me* because I'm Jewish?

WARD. *Objection,* Your Honor.

VOICE OF COURT/ACTOR EIGHT. Sustained.

RUARK. *Yes or no,* Mr. Parmenter.

PARMENTER. Yes.

(*MUSIC: "Purple Heart" by T-Bone Burnett,* [*]
    soft.
*MATHEWS enters and stands upstage of
    Parmenter, watching the testimony.*)

SAVAGE. You were a *convincing liar,* correct?

---

[*] See Production Note on page 165.

PARMENTER. I would say it didn't take too much *convincing* because I had I.D. and there was no one really checking on it. When you sign into a motel under a different name *they* don't put you under the tenth degree.

HALPRIN. Were you a member of the INNER CIRCLE?

WARD. Your Honor, I think that is probably the 50th time I've heard that question.

VOICE OF COURT/ACTOR EIGHT. *60th.*

HALPRIN. I've really racked them up.

SAVAGE. You had to be a convincing liar to get the I.D., didn't you?

PARMENTER. You had to fill out a form.

HALPRIN. Would it be fair to say that you have exhibited during the times you have been drunk and sober a "Jekyll and Hyde" personality?

PARMENTER. There were times when I was drinking that I became violent.

HALPRIN. I take it you're in your "Doctor Jekyll" role today with us?

WARD. *Objection.*

VOICE OF COURT/ACTOR EIGHT. It's stricken. Let's get on with it, Mr. Halprin.

HALPRIN. Last question.

RUARK. We're going to have to rely on you even though you've admitted that you'll *betray your oath* and *betray your friends,* isn't that correct?

MATHEWS. Thus I have no choice.

PARMENTER. Under the situation, that's correct.

MATHEWS. I must stand up like a white man and do battle.

HALPRIN. With Mr. Mathews dead, aren't you the most important living member of The Order?

PARMENTER. That's absurd.

HALPRIN. No further questions.

(*LIGHTS shift to shafts of LIGHT, on MATHEWS and PARMENTER as the BOY runs on, tossing a football in the air.*
LIGHTS crossfade to LIGHTS on ACTOR TWO, ACTOR FOUR and ACTOR SIX as THEY question the BOY.
LIGHTS out on MATHEWS and PARMENTER.
MUSIC fades.)

ACTOR TWO. What should an Order member carry at all times?

BOY. An Order member should carry $500 cash with him at all times.

ACTOR SIX. What numbers should he know?

BOY. He should know the Bear Trap number. He should only call this number if his cover is blown and he is arrested.

ACTOR FOUR. What other numbers should he know?

BOY. He should know the Message Center number. He should only leave messages for other members between four and five p.m. Mountain Standard Time.

ACTOR TWO. Who will relay the messages?

BOY. Carlos.

ACTOR FOUR. Who is Carlos?

BOY. Robert Mathews.

ACTOR FOUR. Where did his name come from?

BOY. From Carlos Sanchez, the man who disposed of the Jew athletes at the Munich Olympics.

ACTOR SIX. What are phones to an Order member?

BOY. Phones are poison. They are monitored by ZOG.

ACTOR TWO. Should a member give out his phone number?

BOY. Only in code. One digit above the actual number.

ACTOR FOUR. What is the number 537-2549?

BOY. (*Tossing Actor Four the football.*) It is 426-1438.

ACTOR TWO. What words should not be used on the phone?

BOY. Right-wing. Guns. Feds. Money. Dollars. Agents. Warrants.

ACTOR SIX. Why?

BOY. ZOG is listening. There is always a more discreet word that can be substituted.

ACTOR FOUR. How does an Order member confuse ZOG?

BOY. He makes two misleading phone calls each week to various parts of the country, then hangs up. ZOG will have to use extra manpower to follow these false leads.

ACTOR SIX. Personality conflicts.

BOY. All personality conflicts must come to an immediate end. If you do not have something positive to say about a comrade, then say nothing at all.

ACTOR FOUR. Alcohol.

BOY. The over-consumption of alcohol is a security risk, it lowers morale, and it will not be tolerated.

ACTOR TWO. If ZOG launches an offensive against The Order, what should be done?

BOY. Inflict maximum damage. Go for the brain, not the foot. Go for the throat, not the hand. An individual Aryan Warrior is capable of inflicting great harm to ZOG.

ACTOR SIX. How does a man become an Aryan Warrior?

BOY. By earning one full point under the Point System.

ACTOR TWO. How are points earned?

BOY. Assassinating members of Congress – one-fifth of a point; Judges – one-sixth; FBI agents and Federal Marshals – one-tenth; journalists and local politicians – one-twelfth.

ACTOR TWO. Is there a way to earn a full point?

BOY. Yes. By assassinating the President of the United States.

ACTOR SIX. What is the ultimate end of politics?

BOY. The ultimate end of politics is war.

ACTOR FOUR. (*Tossing the football back to the Boy.*) And whose country is this?

BOY. This is God's country which he has given to me.

(*MUSIC: "Talkin' Bout a Revolution"* by Tracy Chapman.*

LIGHTS shift as ACTOR ONE, ACTOR THREE, ACTOR FIVE and ACTOR EIGHT, led by ACTOR TEN, rush onstage from various directions. All wear camouflaged fatigues and carry weapons. THEY execute a guerilla warfare maneuver in which they "take" the stage.

The BOY backs away, watching. The WOMEN leave the stage.

RADER watches the maneuver, proudly, then moves to the center bench. HALPRIN approaches him.

The other MEN settle into positions around the perimeter of the stage. THEY clean weapons, remove backpacks, etc.

MUSIC fades.)

---

* See Production Note on page 165.

HALPRIN. Mr. Rader, why did you join CSA — the Covenant, Sword and Arm of the Lord?

RADER. I liked the idea of not being around smoking, drinking and cussing.

VOICE OF ACTOR FOUR. (*On mike.*) Randall Rader. One of the government's original 23 defendants who agreed to testify against his former Order members.

HALPRIN. That's the sole reason you joined?

RADER. Yeah, I'd say so.

VOICE OF ACTOR FOUR. As a survivalist instructor, Rader once killed and ate his own dog to make a point.

HALPRIN. It had nothing to do with religion?

RADER. Well, yes.

HALPRIN. I mean, you could be an *atheist* and not smoke, drink or cuss.

RADER. Well, true. I enjoyed the Christian atmosphere.

HALPRIN. I see. Well, then, what possessed you to participate in arson in 1979?

RADER. I was guided by Mr. Ellison during that.

HALPRIN. Were you assured by Mr. Ellison that that was a Christian act?

RADER. Yes, sir.

HALPRIN. And it was a deliberate burning down of a building to cheat an insurance company, wasn't it?

RADER. Yes, sir.

HALPRIN. Did you question as to how that particular act managed to fit into the teachings of Christ?

RADER. Not at the time.

HALPRIN. I see. If Mr. Ellison assured you it was Christian, why, that was good enough for you?

RADER. Yes, sir.

(*The MEN, led by ACTOR ONE, begin a series of hand-to-hand combat maneuvers involving their weapons.*)

VOICE OF ACTOR FOUR. Rader left the CSA compound in Arkansas in May of 1984 after being recruited by Robert Mathews to come to northern Idaho.

LEATHERMAN. (*Enters.*) You had value in terms of being able to teach people about military groups and shooting guns and all that sort of thing, is that right?

RADER. Yes.

LEATHERMAN. Isn't it true that when you were recruited to join, you were considered the foremost civilian person in this country on the subject of para-military training?

RADER. Some people considered me that.

LEATHERMAN. You did have a certain amount of power, did you not?

RADER. I was given a group to work with, yes.

LEATHERMAN. And you wanted the power, didn't you?

RADER. I enjoyed it to a certain extent, yes.

(Three huge photos appear upstage: Menacham Begin, Jesse Jackson, and Henry Kissinger.
The MEN take positions and begin firing at the photos.
A CACOPHONY OF GUNSHOTS – on tape – underscores the following.)

VOICE OF FOUR. Rader constructed what was called a "Silhouette City" for The Order. Shacks made of wood and cardboard which symbolized an urban environment. Photos of the group's enemies were nailed to the shacks and used as targets.

HALPRIN. What is the maximum number of people you had in your training camp in Idaho?

RADER. Eighteen, I think. Something like that.

HALPRIN. And among the types of training was guerrilla warfare?

RADER. Yes, sir.

HALPRIN. Against whom?

RADER. We did not train against anyone, sir.

HALPRIN. Well, who were you proposing to utilize this *against?*

RADER. Who was *I* proposing?

HALPRIN. Yes.

RADER. The communists.

HALPRIN. Which communists?

RADER. The Russians.

HALPRIN. Any particular *date* in mind?

RADER. No, sir.

HALPRIN. You didn't have any particular target in mind except the invading Russian army, whenever they get here?

RADER. Yes, sir.

(The GUNSHOTS end.
LIGHTS out on the photos.
The MEN sit, relax, drink from canteens, etc.
    ACTOR TEN studies a map. ACTOR ONE is filing a serial number off his weapon, a MAC-10.)

LEATHERMAN. Did you think, as a result of the training that you were providing people, that they were going to commit crimes?

RADER. I thought it was a possibility, yes.

LEATHERMAN. You thought it was *likely to happen,* didn't you?

RADER. Yes.

LEATHERMAN. There was no way you could hide from that fact, could you?

RADER. What do you mean hide from it?

LEATHERMAN. There was no way you could pretend that all this was just *innocent playing in the woods,* was there?

RADER. No.

LEATHERMAN. You *knew*, or had good reason to *think*, that what you were teaching people might be used in such a way that either they or innocent people might get killed?

RADER. Yes.

LEATHERMAN. And yet you went ahead and taught them, right?

RADER. Yes.

HALPRIN. Now, about this MAC-10 that you had originally purchased in your name, it would fire how many rounds a minute?

RADER. About nine hundred.

LEATHERMAN. It would discharge 30 shots in approximately how much time?

RADER. About two seconds, if you stayed on the trigger.

LEATHERMAN. It would empty them in a hurry, right?

RADER. Yes.

HALPRIN. When did you sell that?

RADER. Around May 14th.

HALPRIN. Now, at that time you wanted the serial numbers removed?

RADER. Yes, sir.

HALPRIN. Why?

RADER. Because it was a fully automatic weapon.

HALPRIN. If nothing is going to be *done* with it, what difference does it make?

RADER. If it was found, it could be traced back to me, and I would have to account for why it was fully automatic.

HALPRIN. Did you know what was going to be done with the weapon?

RADER. *No, sir.*

LEATHERMAN. This wasn't a weapon that you would go hunting birds with, was it?

RADER. No.

LEATHERMAN. And you sure wouldn't go hunting squirrels with it, would you?

RADER. No.

LEATHERMAN. Because you'd just — your target would just *disappear* on you, right?

RADER. Yes.

(*ACTOR ONE gives ACTOR TEN the weapon he has been filing. ACTOR TEN and ACTOR THREE exit. The other MEN remain.*)

HALPRIN. Now, when did you say you saw Mr. Mathews and a few other people drive off to Denver?

RADER. That was around the 14th or 15th of June.

HALPRIN. And did you see them taking your weapon with them?

RADER. No, sir.

HALPRIN. Did you *know* they were taking it?

RADER. I was *told* they were.

LEATHERMAN. I mean, the basic value of this type of weapon is that it will shoot out a lot of bullets in a minimal space of time, covering a wide area?

RADER. That's one of the values.

HALPRIN. Now, at that time you knew there was an assassination Step, didn't you?

RADER. Yes, sir.

HALPRIN. And you *knew* they were taking your weapon with them to Denver, right?

RADER. Yes, sir.

LEATHERMAN. What you do with the thing is you *shoot people* with it, right?

RADER. Yes.

HALPRIN. Didn't you know they were going to Denver to kill somebody?

RADER. No, sir.

HALPRIN. You hadn't the *faintest idea,* is that your testimony?

RADER. *Yes, sir.*

HALPRIN. And you saw them come back, didn't you?

RADER. Yes, sir.

HALPRIN. And they had your weapon with them, didn't they?

RADER. I didn't *see it.*

HALPRIN. When did they come back?

RADER. Around the 21st or 22nd of June.

HALPRIN. And is that when you first found out that *Mr. Berg had been eliminated?*

RADER. Yes, sir.

HALPRIN. One more thing. How do you think God feels about your activities?

RADER. (*Pause.*) I think he's pretty aggravated.

HALPRIN.   LEATHERMAN.
No further   That's all.
questions.

(*MUSIC: Wagner's "The American Centennial March."*
The MEN onstage – ACTOR ONE, ACTOR FIVE and ACTOR EIGHT – rise to their feet. THEY have removed their shirts or jackets to reveal green T-shirts with a pattern of five white stars in a circle. In large letters, inside the circle, is inscribed: Northwest Mountain Republic.
A huge banner, identical to the Men's T-shirts, unfurls upstage – covering the three photos.
MUSIC CONTINUES, under.)

ACTOR EIGHT. There exists only one large territory in North America that is as yet white and uncrowded – the five northwest states.

ACTOR FIVE. Washington, Oregon –

ACTOR EIGHT. Idaho –

ACTOR ONE. Montana and Wyoming.

ACTOR FIVE. Our forefathers created the greatest of cultures in lands which offered far less.

ACTOR ONE. In the last decade, tens of thousands of white families have already fled from the mongrelized areas to the northwest.

ACTOR SIX. (*In shaft of LIGHT, holding a book.*) January, 1986. Legislators in 48 states receive a book called *Amendment to the Constitution: Averting the Decline and Fall of America.* The book outlines what is called the Pace Amendment to the Constitution.

ACTOR EIGHT. "No person shall be a citizen of the United States unless he is a non-Hispanic White of the European race —"

ACTOR FIVE. "In whom there is no ascertainable trace of Negro blood —"

ACTOR ONE. "Nor more than one-eighth Mongolian, Asian, Asia Minor, Middle-Eastern, Semitic, Near-Eastern, American Indian, Malaysian or other non-European or non-White blood—"

ACTOR FIVE. "And providing that he is, in appearance, *indistinguishable* from Americans whose ancestral home is the British Isles or northwestern Europe."

ACTOR EIGHT. "Only citizens shall have the right and privilege to reside permanently in the United States."

ACTOR ONE. The Indians have their reservations. We want OUR land.

ACTOR SIX. "James O. Pace" is the pseudonym for the Amendment's author, whose true identity is unknown.

ACTOR FIVE. We don't want to be greedy.

ACTOR ONE. Five states are enough.

ACTOR SIX. Officials at Harvard Law School, however, have verified that the author was a member of the Board of Editors at their International Law Journal. (*LIGHTS out on ACTOR SIX.*)

ACTOR FIVE. (*As HE exits.*) It's a truly Christian gesture.

ACTOR ONE. (*As HE exits.*) It will be a new Garden of Eden.

ACTOR EIGHT. When we take over, we won't ask anyone to leave — but if I was a Jew in Seattle, I'd move to Israel.

(*MUSIC swells.*
LIGHTS shift to JUDITH BERG, seated at the center bench.
ALAN BERG sits at his radio console, in dim LIGHT, watching the testimony.
MUSIC fades.)

VOICE OF ACTOR SEVEN (*On mike.*). State your full name for the record and spell your last name.

JUDITH. My name is Judith Lee Berg. B-e-r-g.

MUELLER. Mrs. Berg, were you married to Alan Berg for 20 years?

JUDITH. I was.

MUELLER. From when to when?

JUDITH. From 1958 to 1978.

MUELLER. Did you have dinner with him on the last day of his life, on June 18th, 1984?

JUDITH. I did.

(Shafts of LIGHT on WARD and MARTINEZ.
SLIDE: THOMAS MARTINEZ
*   FORMER ORDER MEMBER)*

WARD. Mr. Martinez, in January of 1984 did you receive a visit from Robert Mathews?

MARTINEZ. Yes.

WARD. At Philadelphia?

MARTINEZ. Yes.

WARD. Can you tell us what topics were discussed?

MARTINEZ. Well, Bob was pretty upset. He was real tense. I asked him what was wrong and he told me that somebody was causing problems and just, you know, stuff had to be *done*. And he went on with his rhetoric about the Jews and the blacks and everything about his country – and in that conversation he mentioned to keep my eyes and ears open because a guy in Colorado is going to be killed.

(LIGHTS shift to BACKLIGHT on MARTINEZ.)

MUELLER. Your marriage ended in 1978, is that correct?

JUDITH. Yes.

MUELLER. After your marriage ended, did you and Alan Berg remain close friends?

JUDITH. We did.

MUELLER. From time to time would you call in and participate in his programs?

JUDITH. Yes. We'd set up an issue where there were situations going on in the country — as in Johnny Carson's wife wanted twenty thousand dollars for phone calls and Alan always had settlements, and so forth. I would call in and he would do bits on that.

MUELLER. This was prearranged?

JUDITH. Yes.

MUELLER. Did you also have one show in which you had a so-called dispute with Mr. Berg over custody of the dog?

JUDITH. Yes, custody of the dog.

(*Shaft of LIGHT on ANATH WHITE.*
SLIDE: ANATH WHITE
    PRODUCER
    KOA RADIO
    DENVER)

ANATH WHITE. A whole range of things. From very serious pro-and-con kinds of things to fun ones. We would do some frivolous things.

WARD. Such as?

ANATH WHITE. The dating show. He had a garage sale he did periodically. A parrot one time was —

WARD. Like a parrot bird?

ANATH WHITE. A bird. Had evidently been the only witness to a murder in Chicago, and was parroting what had happened in this apartment. The Judge had not yet decided whether this evidence could be admitted into court. Alan opened the lines and asked people to give their view. It was an excellent show.

WARD. Afterwards I will ask you if the parrot got to testify.

(*LIGHTS shift to BACKLIGHT on ANATH WHITE.*
Shaft of LIGHT on PARMENTER.)

MUELLER. Mr. Parmenter, what did Mr. Mathews tell you with respect to the murder?

PARMENTER. He told me about the surveillance. That it was done prior to the murder by an old lady who was a relative of Zillah.

MUELLER. Who was Zillah?

PARMENTER. Zillah was his girlfriend.

MUELLER. What's her last name?

PARMENTER. Craig.

MUELLER. And what do you mean by surveillance?

PARMENTER. This person had gone and done surveillance of his home, his place of employment, his routine.

*(LIGHTS   shift   to   BACKLIGHT   on
      PARMENTER.*
Shaft of LIGHT on CONNOR.
SLIDE: PATRICK CONNOR
      PROMOTION ASSISTANT
      KOA RADIO
      DENVER)

WARD. Did you recall a conversation you had with a visitor at KOA?

CONNOR. Yes, I do.

WARD. Can you describe the person that you met?

CONNOR. A woman, about five-six, middle-aged. Shoulder length hair, dark with gray.

WARD. What did she say to you?

CONNOR. She said she was a student from Wyoming and needed some information. She asked who was on the air and I gave her our lineup.

WARD. Who was on the air at the time this woman was there?

CONNOR. Alan Berg.

WARD. Did she ask you any other questions?

CONNOR. Yes. She asked if everybody had to be buzzed in and out and I said yes.

WARD. Did she ask to meet anyone?

CONNOR. She asked if she could meet Alan Berg. I said no.

WARD. Why?

CONNOR. Because our policy is no one meets or even takes tours of the studios without being cleared through the program director. She thanked me. I said, "You're welcome," and I went back into the studios to get my keys and my coat so I could go to lunch.

WARD. When you came out to go to lunch, did you see anything unusual?

CONNOR. Yes, I did.

WARD. What did you see?

CONNOR. Someone was taking pictures.

WARD. Who?

CONNOR. The woman I had talked to in the lobby.

(*LIGHTS out on WARD, CONNOR, PARMENTER, ANATH WHITE and MARTINEZ.*)

VOICE OF ACTOR ONE. (*On mike.*) June 18th, 1984. Armed with the intelligence provided by Jean Craig, Order members Mathews, Pierce, Lane and Richard Scutari assemble in Denver.

MUELLER. On June 18th, which is a Monday, correct?

(*JUDITH nods.*)

MUELLER. Where did you and Mr. Berg have dinner?

JUDITH. A restaurant called the Jefferson 440. I met Alan — I had my parents' car — and I met him at the Cherry Creek shopping center, about 10, 15 minutes east of Denver. I met him there and we went in his car.

MUELLER. Can you recall what time you went to dinner?

JUDITH. Between 6:30 and 7:00.

(MUSIC: "Prelude Number Two for Piano" by George Gershwin,* very softly underscoring the following.)

MUELLER. Okay. After you had finished dinner, what did you and Mr. Berg do?

JUDITH. We were going home to feed the dog and call his mother.

BERG. (Looking at Judith.) And then we were to visit a friend of ours.

JUDITH. We decided Alan better not because he had to get ready for the next day's show.

MUELLER. At this point you are still in Mr. Berg's car after dinner?

JUDITH. Right. He said —

BERG. We'll call mother tomorrow and won't get Fred all excited and jumping around.

MUELLER. Who is Fred?

JUDITH. The dog.

---

* See Production Note on page 165.

MUELLER. Did you actually stop and buy dog food?

BERG. We did.

JUDITH. We stopped at a convenience store on 6th Avenue, and then he took me to my car.

MUELLER. On the way to your car you drove past Mr. Berg's house?

BERG. Right.

MUELLER. At one point you were actually thinking of going in there yourself?

JUDITH. Yes.

MUELLER. When you drove past Mr. Berg's house did you notice anything unusual?

JUDITH. I did not notice anything unusual.

MUELLER. How long did it take you to get to the Cherry Creek shopping center?

JUDITH. About ten minutes.

MUELLER. And did you pick up your car there?

JUDITH. I did.

MUELLER. And where did you go?

JUDITH. I went to a friend of ours, Bobby Cook.

MUELLER. And where was Mr. Berg going when he left you?

JUDITH. He was going to prepare for the next day's show. And then I was going to call him to make sure I got there all right.

MUELLER. Now, how long a drive from the shopping center back to Mr. Berg's house?

BERG. About ten minutes.

MUELLER. And how long a drive from the shopping center to Bobby's house where *you* were going?

JUDITH. Twenty to twenty-five minutes.

MUELLER. So, if he went straight home he would have gotten there before you got where you were going?

JUDITH. Absolutely.

MUELLER. Did you go to Bobby's?

JUDITH. I did.

MUELLER. And you had made arrangements to call Mr. Berg?

JUDITH. Yes. I went in and I said – I've got to call Alan right away because he's concerned that I would get here all right. So I called and the tape was on.

MUELLER. What tape are you referring to?

JUDITH. Alan had an answering machine.

MUELLER. So nobody answered the phone?

JUDITH. At first I thought maybe he had walked Fred and I kept calling and calling. But he never answered.

(LIGHTS out on JUDITH and MUELLER.
BERG comes out from behind his radio console.
SLIDE: "60 MINUTES"
* CBS*
* JANUARY, 1984)*

VOICE OF ACTOR EIGHT. (*On mike.*) But what are the people who listen to call-in shows actually hearing? Those who listen to Alan Berg get a mixed bag of mayhem and malarkey, political science and pop psychology, common law and uncommon sense — all of it laced with aggression, abuse and sarcasm.

BERG. A woman filed a lawsuit against me early in my career. I think it was the second year I was in the business. Her husband had a coronary while he was listening to my show, so she filed suit against me because he became so angry listening to my show that she felt I was the *causal connection* for the death!

VOICE OF ACTOR EIGHT. Isn't there something a little dangerous about this kind of broadcasting?

BERG. There is a danger. I agree with you. I think that's the danger we exhibit in all free — all rights of free expression, be it columnists who write for newspapers —

VOICE OF ACTOR EIGHT. Yeah, indeed. But you say yourself, you often go on there and you don't know quite what you're going to say.

BERG. Hopefully my legal training will prevent me from saying the one thing that will kill me.

(*MUSIC: "See That My Grave is Kept Clean" by Bob Dylan,* final verse.

---

* See Production Note on page 165.

LIGHTS out on BERG.
LIGHTS reveal the graveyard, as before. The
  WOMEN arrive, shining FLASHLIGHTS, as
  before.
Song ends.)

ACTOR FOUR. (*Turns and speaks to the*
audience.) I am at a party. A sturdy house in an
alabaster city. The ceiling is held up with
perfume and smoke. The conversations are laced
with exclamation points, but the sentences are
missing.

In a corner is a suited man, with a huge
forehead and ill-fitting teeth. He has told a joke.
The joke is off-color and I am off-balance and the
room is oddly caught up in him. He is the kind of
man that when he opens a door, someone finds
him a chair. His joke floats like smoke over the
room and is inhaled like ether.

(*ACTOR TWO and ACTOR SIX turn and look at*
  ACTOR FOUR. THEY recite their respective
  lists of names very softly under the
  following.)

ACTOR FOUR.	ACTOR TWO.	ACTOR SIX.
I move to the kitchen and	Charles Lee Austin.	Michael Harris.

open the
fridge. The
joke is there
next to the
milk. The
cabbage is
laughing
 and
nudging the
cheese.
An avocado
guffaws.
I move to the
bathroom
and the hand
towels are
in hysterics.
My hosts —
the chimney
sweep and
his wife —
are taking a
milk bath
and reading
*The Late
Great Planet
Earth*. The
kleenex is
wiping its
eyes. I move

William
Alan
Rogers.
Scott Adam
Walker.
Roger L.
Morton.
Michael
Schmidt.

Lyle Dean
Nash.
Floyd Shaw.

Billie
Salisbury.
Scott
William
Allgood.
David
Zimmerman
Mark
Edward
Raymond.
Ann Payne.

Patrick
LaRouche.
Charles Lee
Austin.

Monte Ross
Sharpe

Richard
Black.
Steve J.
Lewis.
Bette
Wilder.

Patrick
Deberio.
Richard
O'Connor.
Richard
Jennings.
Eric
Hartman.

Gladys
Engstrom.
Mathew
Mark
Samuels.
Tom D.
Benjamin.
Pat Stone.

Michael
Harris.

to a bedroom
and turn on
a TV. The
weatherman
is howling
with glee, his
veins
bursting his
neck. He is
writing the
JOKE with
his black
marker
across the
continental
United
States.
Across the
room, a baby
sleeps on a
king-sized
bed. As I
lean close to
see its face —
the bed opens
its mouth
and laughs.
A light bulb
snickers

William
Alan
Rogers.
Scott Adam
Walker.
Roger L.
Morton.
Michael
Schmidt.
Lyle Dean
Nash.
Floyd Shaw.

Billie
Salisbury.
Scott
William
Allgood.
David
Zimmerman
Mark
Edward
Raymond.
Ann Payne.

Patrick
LaRouche.
Charles Lee
Austin.

Monte Ross
Sharpe.

Richard
Black.
Steve J.
Lewis.
Bette
Wilder.
Patrick
Deberio.
Richard
O'Connor.
Richard
Jennings.
Eric
Hartman.

Gladys
Engstrom.
Mathew
Mark
Samuels.
Tom D.
Benjamin.
Pat Stone.

Michael
Harris.

ACTOR FOUR.	ACTOR TWO.	ACTOR SIX.
and flickers out. The baby is gone. I race back into the main room and the laughter has subsided.	William Alan Rogers. Scott Adam Walker. Roger L. Morton. Michael Schmidt.	Monte Ross Sharpe. Richard Black. Steve J. Lewis. Bette Wilder.

(ACTOR TWO and ACTOR SIX are silent, staring at ACTOR FOUR.)

ACTOR FOUR. Waiters in tuxedos carry silver trays. On the silver trays are construction helmets with our names monogrammed on the front. I take mine, place it on my head, and accept a refill of burgundy. As we stand at the party, clustered in groups of threes and fours . . . it begins to rain appendages. Arms . . . and legs . . . and feet . . .and hands . . . bounce off our hard hats and come to rest in the plush pile carpeting. Conversations continue, unabated. The suited man with ill-fitting teeth has caught a finger in his wine. We smile and tastefully reward him with golf applause. He steps to the center of the room as the appendages pile up around him. He is, he says, reminded of another joke.

(*ACTOR TWO and ACTOR SIX begin their lists again, softly.*)

ACTOR FOUR. We lean forward to listen as the rain continues to fall, the bones beating on the bones.

(*LIGHTS shift to the BOY standing upstage. He wears a red robe identical to the robe Pastor One wore at the end of Act I. The hood covers his face.*
The WOMEN leave, reciting their lists.
The SOUND of a low droning underscores the following.
During the following, the BOY moves downstage and discovers a small shrine. HE removes his robe and hood — revealing him to be dressed in camouflaged fatigues. HE inspects the following items which comprise the shrine: a copy of Mein Kampf, *a framed photograph of Adolph Hitler, a Nazi armband, and a MAC-10. HE puts the armband on and lifts the weapon, ready for battle.*)

ACTOR NINE. (*In shaft of LIGHT.*) October, 1984. Several events lead to the unraveling of The Order.

ACTOR EIGHT. (*In shaft of LIGHT.*) A submachine gun which Robert Mathews mistakenly left behind at the site of the Ukiah robbery is traced to its owner, Andrew Barnhill — a known Order member.

ACTOR NINE. The FBI suspects for the first time that the numerous crimes are the work of one group.

ACTOR EIGHT. Thomas Martinez is arrested in Philadelphia for passing counterfeit money. Still a trusted friend of Robert Mathews, Martinez agrees to be an FBI informant — enabling the FBI to track the movements of The Order.

ACTOR NINE. October 18, 1984. Federal agents arrive at Gary Yarbrough's house in Sandpoint, Idaho. Yarbrough opens fire on the agents and flees.

ACTOR EIGHT. A search of Yarbrough's house uncovers a huge cache of weapons, explosives and documents revealing the Command Structure of The Order.

ACTOR NINE. Also discovered is a shrine to Adolph Hitler.

ACTOR EIGHT. November 24, 1984. Using Mathews as a decoy, the FBI tracks Yarbrough and Mathews to a motel in Portland, Oregon. Yarbrough is captured. Mathews escapes after a shootout with FBI agents.

(LIGHTS reveal MATHEWS, dressed for battle, his hand bandaged. The BOY moves next to him.
LIGHTS out on ACTOR EIGHT, ACTOR NINE and the shrine.)

MATHEWS. After running for two blocks, I decided to quit being the hunted and become the hunter. I drew my gun and waited behind a concrete wall for the agent to draw near. When I aimed my gun at the head of the closest agent . . . I saw the handsome face of a young white man . . . and lowered my aim to his knee and foot. Had I not done so, I could have killed both agents and still had left the use of my hand — which is now mangled beyond repair. That is the last time I will ever give quarter.

(MATHEWS places a pendant, identical to his own, around the BOY'S neck. Then MATHEWS and the BOY, holding their weapons, turn and face the audience.)

VOICE OF ACTOR EIGHT. *(On mike.)* Following word of the shootout in Portland, Order members flee to various parts of the country.

VOICE OF ACTOR NINE. *(On mike.)* Many take refuge at the Arkansas compound of the Covenant, Sword and Arm of the Lord.

VOICE OF ACTOR EIGHT. Mathews and four others flee to Whidbey Island, near Seattle.

VOICE OF ACTOR NINE. A Declaration of War is drafted and signed.

MATHEWS. WE HEREBY DECLARE OURSELVES TO BE A FREE AND SOVEREIGN PEOPLE. LET FRIEND AND FOE ALIKE BE MADE AWARE.

BOY. WE DECLARE OURSELVES TO BE IN A FULL AND UNRELENTING STATE OF WAR WITH THOSE FORCES SEEKING AND PROMOTING THE DESTRUCTION OF OUR FAITH AND OUR RACE.

MATHEWS. FOR BLOOD, SOIL AND HONOR, FOR THE FUTURE OF OUR CHILDREN –

BOY. FOR OUR KING, JESUS CHRIST –

MATHEWS. WE COMMIT OURSELVES TO BATTLE.

VOICE OF ACTOR NINE. One critical piece of evidence is found at Gary Yarbrough's house in Sandpoint.

BOY. NEVER FORGET:

VOICE OF ACTOR NINE. It is a fully automatic MAC-10 submachine gun.

BOY. AS LONG AS ONE MEMBER OF THE ORDER IS ALIVE, THE ORDER LIVES.

VOICE OF ACTOR EIGHT. The gun that five months earlier had murdered Alan Berg.

(*LIGHTS shift to BERG at the radio console, talking to one of HIS favorite callers.*
JUDITH BERG watches him from upstage.

The droning SOUND fades out.)

BERG. 861-TALK. 861-8255. You're on the air.

VOICE OF ACTOR FOUR. (*On mike.*) I expect you to hang up on me. You are the great humanitarian who makes people miserable three hundred and sixty-five days a year.

BERG. It shows what masochists people are when you look at what I've done in talk radio. If people have such a need to listen all the time, they must have an *enormous* need to be masochistic. Why are you listening now?

VOICE OF ACTOR FOUR. I'm listening —

BERG. Also, considering I'm *not on the air* three hundred and sixty-five days a year, you don't count well.

VOICE OF ACTOR FOUR. That's right.

BERG. Unless you play *tapes* of my show on the weekends to *make* yourself miserable. *I* don't stay tuned to anything *I* don't like. You really have a problem.

VOICE OF ACTOR FOUR. I do. I do. I agree with that.

BERG. Perhaps I could help you through this grief you're experiencing —

VOICE OF ACTOR FOUR. I'm not experiencing grief —

BERG. What is the *point* you're making? Why do you listen to me?

VOICE OF ACTOR FOUR. I don't, Alan, I *don't.*

BERG. Oh, darling, I don't think you've missed a show I've done for the last seven years I've been in the business. You're always there and you always know what I've done.

JUDITH. (*Moves to the center bench as SHE speaks.*) At first I thought maybe he had walked Fred, and I kept calling and calling, but he never answered. In between calling him, I called my mother, just to tell her, you know, where I was and that I wouldn't be home that late. Then, later, since she knew where I was, my mother called and she asked Bobby what I was doing. Bobby said we were just sitting there, I was trying to get a hold of Alan. And she said, "Is the television on?" And Bobby said no. And she told her what had happened.

ACTOR TEN. (*In shaft of LIGHT, still dressed as MATHEWS.*) June 18, 1984. 9:20 p.m. Bruce Pierce waits in the bushes which surround the driveway of Alan Berg's home at 1445 Adams Street in Denver. David Lane waits nearby in a getaway car. Also in the vicinity, in separate vehicles, are Robert Mathews and Richard Scutari. Berg pulls into the driveway in his black Volkswagon. He lights a cigarette. He grabs a small bag of dog food he has purchased. And he begins to step out of the car.

(*MUELLER in a shaft of LIGHT.*)

*The following witnesses each walk into the same
     shaft of LIGHT, give their testimony, and
     leave.*
BERG and ACTOR TEN watch the testimony.
JUDITH BERG remains lit as well.)

MS. WIGGINS. It was a loud neighborhood.
Loud is probably one of the most striking things
about that neighborhood.

MUELLER. Were you at home that evening?

MS. WIGGINS. Yes.

MUELLER. And do you remember hearing
an unusual sound?

MS. WIGGINS. I thought it sounded like a
machine gun, but it was too quiet. Maybe a whole
package of firecrackers going.

MUELLER. Mr. Parmenter, did you discuss
with Mr. Pierce the killing of Alan Berg?

PARMENTER. Yes, I did.

MUELLER. What did Mr. Pierce say to you?

PARMENTER. He told me Berg fell as if the
carpet had been pulled out from under him.

MUELLER. Now, Office Phelan, when you got
there, was the body and the blood which is depicted
in that photograph different in any way?

OFFICE PHELAN. (*Holding an 8 x 10.*) I
recall that the right leg of the victim was still
inside the vehicle. Also, this picture shows the
blood a little further advanced down the driveway
than when I first arrived. And, when I arrived on

the scene, there was a burning cigarette to the right of the victim's body.

MUELLER. Detective Kerber, can you identify what is contained in Exhibit 30-37?

DETECTIVE KERBER. (*Holding a small plastic bag containing bullets.*) Yes. These are three .45 caliber bullets I recovered at the morgue.

MUELLER. When did you first notice them?

DETECTIVE KERBER. We were running the video, and I was taking photographs, and as they turned the body – they fell out of the body.

MUELLER. *They fell out of the body?*

DETECTIVE KERBER. Yes.

MUELLER. Doctor Ogura, you are the coroner's pathologist for the city of Denver?

DOCTOR OGURA. (*Holding a clipboard.*) Yes.

MUELLER. Doctor Ogura, from your examination, is it possible to say, conclusively, exactly how many bullets hit Alan Berg that night?

DOCTOR OGURA. No. I am not positive how many. But at the time of the examination, when I had finished, I felt that a minimum of 12 bullets had to have entered him.

MUELLER. Mr. Martinez, during the time you were cutting counterfeit bills, did you have a conversation with David Lane about the murder of Alan Berg?

MARTINEZ. Yes. We were sitting at the table cutting money. I asked him and he laughed and

he said, "Hell, I drove the getaway car." And I
was in shock, and I said you've got to be kidding
me. He said, "No. We watched that Jew kike
while he was eating dinner — our intelligence
was gathered real well — and we waited for him
for six or seven hours in that area."

MUELLER. Were the words "Jew kike" his
words?

MARTINEZ. Yes.

MUELLER. And what was his tone of voice
when he told you about his participation in this
incident?

MARTINEZ. Just natural.

*(LIGHTS out on MARTINEZ and ACTOR TEN.
Only BERG, MUELLER and JUDITH BERG
    remain lit.)*

BERG. Why turn here? There are thirty-four
other radio stations in this town. Why turn here if
I make you miserable? You have no credibility.
You *dig* what I do. You have a *need*.
Unfortunately, you have no sense of humor.
That's why you can't ever enjoy this show. And
that's why you're a *loser*, as are all people who
have no sense of humor. And you are
categorically one of them! (*Pushes a button. The
LIGHT on HIM snaps out.*)

MUELLER. Mrs. Berg, you were never
successful in reaching Alan?

JUDITH. No.

MUELLER. You had stated that you were going to discuss the next day's show. Do you recall the topic of the next day's show?

JUDITH. Yes. The next day's show would have been gun control.

MUELLER. No further questions.

(LIGHTS out on JUDITH and BERG. MUELLER steps forward.
Shaft of LIGHT on ACTOR FIVE.)

ACTOR FIVE. December 16th, 1985. After three and a half months of testimony, the government's case against The Order goes to the jury in Seattle.

MUELLER. Now, in working on this case this summer it occurred to me that I might be giving an argument some day, and I was thinking about something that I read. I simply want to borrow the words of the speaker, because he described it far better than I can.

ACTOR FIVE. The jury of eight white women and four white men deliberate for two weeks.

MUELLER. The speaker was a young man by the name of Peter Hill, who was one of the hostages on the TWA jet that was hijacked out of Athens and brought to Beirut. This individual, when he got out, made this statement describing the people that captured him: "They were a band of thieves, thugs and murderers who justified their deeds with vows of religious fervor."

ACTOR FIVE. December 30, 1985. A verdict is reached.

MUELLER. I read that and I said to myself: That's the defendants in our case. And I submit to you that is *exactly* what they were and they should be found guilty as charged. Thank you.

ACTOR FIVE. All ten defendants are found guilty of racketeering and of conspiring to racketeer. Sentencing takes place on February 6th, 1986.

(*LANE, YARBROUGH and PIERCE enter. THEY are handcuffed and wear prison fatigues.*)

VOICE OF COURT/ACTOR SIX. (*On mike.*) Mr. Lane, is there anything you'd like to say before sentence is passed?

(*SLIDE: Photo of DAVID LANE, with his name and sentence as a caption.*)

ACTOR FIVE. Pierce and Duey are sentenced to 100 years in prison. Yarbrough and Kemp, 60 years.

LANE. For a time I pondered whether I was going to make any statement. However, I'll probably never have my voice heard outside of the cage again, and I'm going to take this opportunity to say a few things.

ACTOR FIVE. Lane, Barnhill, Craig, Silva, Evans, and McBrearty get 40 years each.

LANE. I do not speak for all members of The Order. I most assuredly am the voice of my dearest friend, the most incredible man I've ever known, the finest man yet produced on this continent: Robert Jay Mathews.

(*A shaft of BACKLIGHT slowly reveals MATHEWS, upstage.*)

ACTOR NINE. (*In shaft of LIGHT.*) December 7th, 1984. Federal agents and local law enforcement personnel surround three houses on Whidbey Island, near Seattle. Shipping lanes on Puget Sound are closed and air traffic is diverted around the area.

ACTOR TWO. (*In shaft of LIGHT.*) The houses are suspected to be the hideout of several Order members, including Robert Jay Mathews.

ACTOR NINE. They are also rumored to be stockpiled with huge quantities of arms, ammunition and explosives.

LANE. When a little man stands alone against something as large as the American branch of the World Government, he has to question his own rightness and sanity – and I have done so.

ACTOR NINE. As the siege at Whidbey Island continues, a Navy helicopter flies over the houses, demanding that the fugitives surrender.

LANE. I have given all that I have and all that I am to waken my people from their sleep of death. And if my efforts were futile, then mankind's dreams to the stars are over.

ACTOR NINE. The first person to emerge from the house is Randy Duey.

ACTOR TWO. Duey runs toward the FBI, brandishing a machine gun. He stops when he sees them and says:

ACTOR NINE. "You're all white men."

ACTOR TWO. At which point he surrenders.

VOICE OF COURT/ACTOR SIX. Mr. Yarbrough.

(SLIDE: Photo of GARY YARBROUGH, with his name and sentence as a caption.)

YARBROUGH. The question is not whether we are guilty, but whether the indictment is LEGAL.

ACTOR NINE. After twenty-four hours, three other Order members surrender on Whidbey Island. Mathews is still believed to be inside one of the houses.

YARBROUGH. This was a political trial, and these men are no more criminals than their forefathers that participated in the Boston Tea Party for the very same cause: unjust laws, unjust taxes, freedom of speech, freedom of religion.

LANE. History.

YARBROUGH. I won't plead to this court for leniency. I will make my pleas to my God and Father.

LANE. History will be my true judge.

YARBROUGH. YOU HAVE NO POWER OVER ME EXCEPT WHAT COMES FROM HIM.

ACTOR NINE. December 8th. 11 a.m. Negotiations break down between Mathews and the FBI.

VOICE OF COURT/ACTOR SIX. Mr. Pierce.

(*SLIDE: Photo of BRUCE PIERCE, with his name and sentence as a caption.*)

ACTOR TWO. The FBI begins firing tear gas cannisters into the house.

PIERCE. I'm not going to waste my time or yours and cry to you, nor beg to this court for mercy. Your mind's made up. I want you to know that the power given you is from Almighty God alone and NO ONE ELSE – and the sentence you impose on me is according to His will on my life.

ACTOR NINE. 3:30 p.m. A single gunshot is fired inside the house.

ACTOR TWO. Thinking Mathews may have taken his own life, a SWAT team enters the house.

BERG. (*In dim LIGHT at his console.*) Let it flow. Let people choose to believe what they want.

YARBROUGH. I miss my family dearly.

BERG. Challenge it in open forums.

ACTOR NINE. Mathews is hiding on the second floor of the house.

PIERCE. I'm sorry for the pain and grief I've caused my dear wife, my family.

YARBROUGH. I would like to be able to hug my children.

ACTOR TWO. Mathews opens fire on the agents.

YARBROUGH. I don't wish for anyone to go through what I have just been through.

ACTOR NINE. Mathews single-handedly drives the agents from the house.

YARBROUGH. But there will be many more to follow.

BERG. I think, short of inciting a riot, let people say things they want to say.

YARBROUGH. The blood will flow and it grieves me.

ACTOR FOUR. Following the Seattle verdict, the Denver district attorney considers filing murder charges in the Berg case.

BERG. As ugly as they may be.

ACTOR FOUR. Unable to get a confession from any of the participants, and fearful of the trial's cost, the Denver authorities drop the case.

BERG. That, to me, is true freedom of speech.

ACTOR FOUR. The members of The Order are indicted, instead, for "violating Alan Berg's civil rights by killing him."

(*MUSIC: A boy's choir singing "The Battle Hymn of the Republic." The song begins very softly, and builds in volume throughout the following.*)

LANE. Not long ago, a little five year-old white girl who calls me Uncle David asked me, "Uncle David, why are you in jail?" And I answered, "Because I love you, and because some bad people don't want little white children to live on earth anymore."

PIERCE. I'd like to bring honor to my family—

YARBROUGH. As ye have judged, so shall ye be judged.

LANE. This tyranny leaves men only two choices:

PIERCE. My brother kinsman —

YARBROUGH. I am free of your blood.

LANE. Life with dishonor —

PIERCE. And glory to God.

LANE. Or death with honor.

YARBROUGH. It's on your own hands.

MATHEWS. THUS I HAVE NO CHOICE.

(*MATHEWS walks downstage. The other ACTORS part. MATHEWS is battle-worn, his hand bandaged. HE carries a submachine gun. The stage grows very dark, except for a shaft of LIGHT on MATHEWS.*

*Simultaneously, a huge American flag begins to
    unfurl. It covers the entire upstage wall.
MUSIC begins to SWELL.)*

MATHEWS. THE GOVERNMENT SEEMS
DETERMINED TO FORCE THE ISSUE. I MUST
STAND UP LIKE A WHITE MAN AND DO
BATTLE.

ACTOR NINE. 6:11 p.m.

MATHEWS. THE DAY WILL COME WHEN
YOU WILL PAY FOR BETRAYING YOUR
RACE.

ACTOR TWO. Fearing Mathews may try to
escape under cover of darkness –

ACTOR NINE. The FBI orders a helicopter to
drop illumination flares on the Whidbey Island
house.

*(The stage, and the theatre, begin to be engulfed in
    brilliant, blinding, red/orange light.)*

MATHEWS. WE HOLD YOU RESPONSIBLE
FOR THESE THINGS:

ACTOR NINE. The flares burn through the
ceiling and fall into the house.

MATHEWS. FOR EVERY WHITE CHILD
TERRORIZED IN A RACIALLY MIXED
SCHOOL.

ACTOR TWO. The flares ignite the
explosives within the house.

MATHEWS. FOR EVERY WHITE PERSON MURDERED IN ONE OF OUR URBAN JUNGLES.

ACTOR NINE. Mathews' arsenal explodes around him.

MATHEWS. FOR EVERY WHITE WOMAN RAPED BY ONE OF THE ARROGANT "EQUALS" ROAMING OUR STREETS.

ACTOR TWO. The house is consumed in flames.

MATHEWS. EACH DAY THE LIST GROWS LONGER, BUT THE DAY WILL COME WHEN THE WHOLE SCORE WILL BE SETTLED AND YOU WILL PAY FOR EVERY ONE OF THESE DEBTS IN FULL.

ACTOR NINE. Mathews is incinerated.

(*LIGHTS out on ACTOR NINE and ACTOR TWO.*)

ACTOR ONE. WHAT YOU SEE TONIGHT—

ACTOR SEVEN. MANY HAVE DISAGREED WITH OUR METHODS.

ACTOR EIGHT. AT LEAST WE WERE NOT AFRAID TO TAKE ON THE BEAST.

ACTOR ONE. WHAT YOU ARE EXPERIENCING TONIGHT –

ACTOR SEVEN. WE HAVE GIVEN YOU TEN MARTYRS.

ACTOR EIGHT. A NEW DAY IS DAWNING FOR WHITE PEOPLE IN THIS COUNTRY.

ACTOR ONE. YOU WILL NEVER AGAIN FORGET.

MATHEWS. WHETHER YOU WERE AN INSTIGATOR OF THE TREASON, OR WHETHER YOU JUST WENT ALONG FOR THE RIDE WILL MAKE LITTLE DIFFERENCE TO US.

ACTOR SEVEN. IT IS TIME TO FOLLOW OUR EXAMPLE.

ACTOR EIGHT. THE ORDER HAS SHOWN YOU THE WAY.

MATHEWS. WHEN THE DAY COMES, WE WILL NOT ASK YOU WHETHER YOU SWUNG TO THE RIGHT OR WHETHER YOU SWUNG TO THE LEFT –

ACTOR SEVEN. SUCCEED WHERE WE FAILED.

MATHEWS. WE WILL SIMPLY SWING YOU FROM THE NECK.

ACTOR ONE. HAIL VICTORY.

MATHEWS, ACTOR SEVEN, ACTOR EIGHT. HAIL VICTORY!

(As MUSIC reaches a CRESCENDO, ZILLAH CRAIG enters, carrying a baby wrapped in a white blanket. SHE walks, ceremonially to MATHEWS. SHE stands before him. Barefoot. Hair down.
MATHEWS extends his arms to receive the child.
ZILLAH CRAIG places the baby in HIS arms.
MUSIC STOPS, ABRUPTLY.

LIGHTS shift, abruptly, to shafts of LIGHT on PARMENTER, BERG, ACTOR FOUR, and MATHEWS standing with ZILLAH, holding their baby.)

ACTOR FOUR. Two months before his death on Whidbey Island, Robert Mathews attends to his mistress, Zillah Craig, as she delivers their child in a secluded farmhouse near Laramie, Wyoming.

PARMENTER. I was a very unstable individual. I was dissatisfied with my life and my circumstances. I was looking for something to give me self-worth, some identity – and the movement itself gave that to me. It gave me something to blame my situation on.

ACTOR FOUR. April 7th, 1988. Fort Smith, Arkansas. A verdict is reached in the trial of 13 leading white supremacists charged with conspiring to overthrow the government and establish a White Homeland in the northwest.

PARMENTER. The change in my views, since my arrest, took time. It didn't happen overnight.

ACTOR FOUR. The Fort Smith defendants, including Richard Butler, Robert Miles, Louis Beam and five members of The Order, are found NOT GUILTY.

PARMENTER. I was given opportunities to read the Bible in its entirety.

ZILLAH. (*To audience.*) Everything has to have its time and its season.

PARMENTER. And it was at that time that I discovered that the Identity Doctrine is a false doctrine.

ACTOR FOUR. Thomas Robb, National Chaplain of the Ku Klux Klan is asked about the Fort Smith verdict.

ZILLAH. Know that the hour of the harvest comes.

ACTOR FOUR. Robb says: "The government was going to send a message to the movement."

ZILLAH. In the right time —

ACTOR FOUR. "The movement sent a message to the government."

ZILLAH. More than just the moon shall rise.

ACTOR FOUR. December, 1988. On the fourth anniversary of his death, a crowd of skinheads and white supremacists gather on Whidbey Island. They demand the island be renamed "Robert Jay Mathews Memorial Park."

(*MUSIC: U2's "In God's Country," from the beginning, soft.*
LIGHTS focus down to reveal only BERG, PARMENTER and MATHEWS.
During the following, MATHEWS slowly lifts the baby toward the sky.)

BERG. (*Simply.*) "Things fall apart. The center cannot hold."

PARMENTER. For the first time in my life I am at peace with myself.

BERG. "Mere anarchy is loosed upon the world."

PARMENTER. And what I am here for is to right a terrible wrong.

BERG. "And everywhere the ceremony of innocence is drowned."

PARMENTER. I consider this a real tragedy in my life —

MATHEWS. Never forget:

PARMENTER. And I'm just trying to correct that.

MATHEWS. As long as one member of The Order is alive —

BERG. "The best lack all conviction, while the worst are full of passionate intensity."

MATHEWS. The Order lives.

(*MUSIC BUILDS STRONGLY as the BOY enters. HE wears camouflaged fatigues, Nazi armband, and the pendant around HIS neck. The BOY carries a memorial cross of flowers. On the cross is a ribbon which reads:* Remember Whidbey Island. *HE stands the wreath at center. HE places his hand over HIS heart.*
A LIGHT *in front of the BOY throws a huge shadow of the cross against the American flag.*
MUSIC STOPS, ABRUPTLY.)

BOY. And to the Republic. For which it stands. One Aryan Nation under God. Indivisible. With Liberty. And Justice. For All.

(*Darkness. Silence.*)

END OF PLAY

PRODUCTION NOTE

A good amplification and sound system is required.

A slide projector and screen are desirable.

If it is impossible or impractical to use slides in a production, the information contained in the slides should be done as Voice Over narration at the point the slides would have been shown. The exceptions to this would be the slides and pictures at the beginning of the play, the series commencing with RICHARD KEMP "HAMMER," following the line, "The government brings racketeering charges against nine men ..." and concluding with "Photo of ROBERT JAY MATHEWS, with his name as a caption;" and the series of three slides near the end, commencing with "Photo of DAVID LANE, with his name and sentence ..." following the line, "Mr. Lane, is there anything you'd like to say ..." and concluding with "Photo of BRUCE PIERCE, WITH HIS NAME AND SENTENCE ..." This information can simply be eliminated.

*Please note:
Mention is made of songs which are *not* in the public domain. Producers of this play are hereby *CAUTIONED* that permission to produce this play does not include rights to use these songs in production. Producers should contact the copyright owners directly for rights, c/o ASCAP or BMI, New York City.

If an ACTOR ELEVEN is added, the cast lising would be changed to read as follows:

ACTOR THREE: AlanBerg

ACTOR TEN: Robert Jay Mathews, martyr, Skinhead.

ACTOR ELEVEN: Mister Jones, (conspiratologist), Ruark, (attorney for Bruce Pierce), Candidate, The Voice of the Court (except where noted).

Additional changes that should be made if an ACTOR ELEVEN is added are as follows:

ACTOR ELEVEN should replace ACTOR THREE in page 16 - 21.

ACTOR ELEVEN should replace ACTOR TEN on page 30.

The following speeches on page 43 & 44 should be reassigned to ACTOR ELEVEN: "Church of the Creator." "Covenant, Sword and Arm of the Lord." "Invisible Empire of the Ku Klux Klan." "National Democratic Front. National Socialist Liberation Front."

ACTOR ELEVEN should replace ACTOR TEN as a CANDIDATE on pages 46 - 51.

ACTOR ELEVEN should replace ACTOR TEN as a CALLER on pages 61 and 62.

ACTOR ELEVEN should replace ACTOR TEN on pages 66 - 75.

ACTOR ELEVEN should replace ACTOR THREE as a CANDIDATE on pages 77 - 87.

ACTOR ELEVEN should replace ACTOR THREE on pages 118 - 124.

The VOICE OF ACTOR ELEVEN should replace the VOICE OF ACTOR EIGHT on pages 136 and 137.

ACTOR ELEVEN should replace ACTOR TEN on pages 147 - 150.

ACTOR ELEVEN should play the VOICE OF THE COURT *throughout*, with the exception of pages 108 - 114. One these pages, the VOICE of THE COURT should be played by ACTOR EIGHT.

COSTUME LIST

ACTOR ONE

Basic: Dark pants, black socks, black shoes, white shirt.
Farrell: "Denver" sweatshirt.
Phillips: Suit jacket, tie.
Pastor One: Light blue shirt with Aryan Nations patch on arm, dark blue tie, dark blue baseball-type cat with patch identical to patch on shirt. (End of Act One - add bright red robe and hood.)
Savage: Suit jacket, tie.
Father: Comfortable, cardigan sweater
Detective Kerber: Overcoat
David Lane: (Act One) Bulky sweater, glasses, camouflage cap. (Act Two) Orange prison jumpsuit, handcuffs. Also camouflage garb, green-shirt with "Northwest Mountain Republic" logo, combat boots.

ACTOR TWO

Basic: Blouse and skirt, raincoat for cemetery scenes.
Leatherman: Dress jacket to match skirt.
Judith Berg: Dress for courtroom scenes.

ACTOR THREE

Basic: Dark pants, light shirt, black socks, black shoes.

Berg: Ascot, cardigan sweater, glasses.

Candidate: Light blue shirt with Aryan Nations arm patch, dark blue tie, dark blue cap with patch identical to patch on shirt.

Mister Jones: Corduroy jacket, sweater vest, sneakers, fishing hat.

Ruark: Three-piece suit, tie.

Also: Camouflage garb, combat boots.

ACTOR FOUR

Basic: Skirt and blouse, raincoat for cemetery scenes.

Mueller: Suit jacket, scarf or brooch for blouse.

Wife of Farmer: Floral print dress, old cardigan sweater, flat shoes.

Also: Studded denim jacket for Caller.

ACTOR FIVE

Basic: Dark pants, light blue shirt (used for Candidate, patch hidden by jacket when Parmenter), dark socks, black shoes.

Parmenter: Dark blue suit coat, sweater vest, tie, handkerchief.

Candidate: Same as Actor Three

Also: "Denver Broncos" cap for Caller, black
     jumpsuit and black ski mask for Ukiah
     robbery. Camouflage garb, green t-shirt with
     "Northwest Mountain Republic" logo, combat
     boots.

ACTOR SIX

Basic: Simple skirt and light blouse, raincoat for
     cemetery scenes.
Zillah Craig: Camisole under cotton shirt, jeans.
     (End of Act One - with skirt, barefoot.)
Student: Jeans, sweatshirt with a University logo,
     sneakers.
Anath White: Dress jacket to match skirt.
Ms. Wiggins: House dress, sandals.
Also: Robe and curlers in hair for Caller.

ACTOR SEVEN

Basic: Dark pants, white shirt, black socks, black
     shoes.
Elliot: Western tie, suit coat.
Ward: Dark blue three-piece suit, tie.
Pastor Two: Dark green suit and tie, Nazi
     armband. (End of Act One --add deep blue
     robe and hood.)
Robinson: Same as Ward.
Randall Rader: Black turtleneck, silver crucifix
     on chain, black jacket.
Dr. Ogura: White lab coat, glasses.

Gary Lee Yarbrough: Orange prison jumpsuit, handcuffs.

Also: Black jumpsuit and black ski mask for Ukiah robbery . Camouflage garb, combat boots.

ACTOR EIGHT

Basic: Dark pants, white shirt, dark socks, black shoes.

Chappel: Suit coat to match pants, tie.

Farmer: Overalls, flannel shirt, denim jacket, feed cap, boots.

Pastor Three: Add suspenders, open collar of shirt, roll up sleeves, handkerchief. (End of Act One--add white robe and hood.)

Peter Lake: Black leather jacket, sunglasses.

Mister Smith: Cardigan sweater, bow tie, worn loafers or slippers.

Thomas Martinez: Camouflage pants, dark turtleneck.

Bruce Pierce: Orange prison jumpsuit, handcuffs.

Also: Camouflage garb, green t-shirt with "Northwest Mountain Republic" logo, combat boots.

ACTOR NINE

Basic: Dark pants, light shirt, dark socks, black shoes.

Halprin: Suitcoat to match pants, tie, glasses (Note: Halprin is younger than the other attorneys in the play, so his choice of clothes and glasses should reflect this.)

Candidate: Same as Actor Three: Overdress this with long black robe, yarmulke and tallith.

Patrick Connor: Light blue shirt, blazer.

Officer Phelan: Dark blue Denver police uniform with badge.

Also: Accessories for Callers. Tan suit for end of Act One - distressed severely for Skinhead scene. Black jumpsuit and black ski mask for Ukiah robbery. Camouflage garb, combat boots.

ACTOR TEN

Basic: Dark, cotton/denim pants, dark t-shirt.

Robert Jay Mathews: Flannel shirt, sweater, glasses, casual shoes. (Later in Act One - camouflage pants, t-shirt, combat boots. (End of Act of One with Zillah - flannel shirt, no t-shirt.

Candidate: Same as Actor Nine.

Skinhead: Torn black jeans, torn t-shirt, leather jacket inscribed with "White Power", worn

boots, knit cap or beret with swastika spray
painted onto it, tattoos (optional).
Also: Bathrobe for Caller. Black jumpsuit and
    black ski mask for Ukiah robbery.
    Camouflage garb, combat boots.

BOY

Basic: Jeans, dark sneakers, cotton shirt and/or
    sweatshirt.
Also: Uniform identical to Pastor One and
    Candidates. Jacket added to Basic for
    cemetery scene. Red robe and hood, when
    noted. Camouflage garb and combat boots,
    when noted.

PROPERTY PLOT

DC Bench
SL Bench
SR Bench
CS Bench
White Candle (perishable) (BOY)
2 - Candles in a 3 candle holder
Weapons (for 5, MAC-10, Uzi, & other automatic
    weapons)
Ammunition belts, holsters (for 5)
Baby bundled in a white blanket
Radio Console w/practical mike and phone bank
Swivel Chair for radio console
Mug of coffee (BERG)
Cigarettes (BERG)
Lighter & matches (BERG)
Ashtray (BERG)
8- 3"x5" cards (w/info about the State of Israel
    (FARRELL & ELLIOTT)
Lawyer paraphernalia (pens/pencils, paper
    binders with clips on top, legal pads)
    (ACTORS 1,2,3,4,7,8,9)
Farmer's small table
Farmer's ladder backed chair
Pile of Newspapers (FARMER'S WIFE)
Pair of Scissors (FARMER'S WIFE)
File box FARMER'S WIFE)
2 mugs of coffee (FARMER & WIFE)
1 Book (*The Turner Diaries*) (MATHEWS)
Small notebook (pocket-sized) (ACTOR TWO)